PRAISE FOR *NATURAL BORN WINNERS*

'*Natural Born Winners* encourages, comforts and supports me to believe in my world. In a realm of frowns and "NO", Robin Sieger becomes your mentor and helps you to remember magic happens, dreams come true and the child inside should always smile. There really is a word of "YES" waiting to be discovered. Thank you Robin.' Joy Collingbourne, student

'Everyone is a natural born winner, it's just that sometimes we forget. I forgot whilst trying to decide whether to return to Everest, as two previous attempts to reach the summit had ended in failure and left me questioning my ability. I was rescued by Robin: his gentle words and effective techniques encouraged me to cast my demons aside and in May 2004 finally summit Mt Everest and realise an ambition that I had nurtured for 17 years.' Paul Deegan, mountaineer and author of *The Mountain Traveller's Handbook*

'It's no good just wanting to succeed. You need to blend work with creativity and the delivery of value. But beyond these strengths you need the timeless principles that Robin shares with you in this great book. Read it and step closer to your potential!' Nick Rampley-Sturgeon, entrepreneur and property millionaire, www.buyingtorent.com

'*Natural Born Winners* is a must read for every start-up entrepreneur, it is packed with real world practical advice. I have given copies to many of my staff and my children and find its simplicity inspirational.' Mike Balfour, founder of Fitness First & UK Entrepreneur of the Year 2001

'Since reading *Natural Born Winners*, I have derived enormous personal benefit by acting on the principles. I use Robin's book extensively in my teaching of Physical Education. The students understand the link between the *Natural Born Winners* ideals and optimising sports performances. Many other students have been inspired by the book and have gained a renewed enthusiasm for their studies and, more importantly, the belief that they have control of their lives.' James Hammond, head of sport, St Antony's RC School, Surrey

'Robin Sieger has the unique gift of being able to relate insightful and relevant real life and business experiences in a way which is motivational, humorous and inspires action. He has added real value to our business and was the catalyst for realising significant, sustainable improvements in our business performance. If I was to recommend one business book it would be *Natural Born Winners*. I know through following its simple personal actions it will support you to deliver a step change in your personal and business performance.' Jim Reeve, MD Zurich IFA Group

'Generally people make "New Year's Resolutions" whereas I choose another read of this book. Each time I gain a new surge of self-confidence, self-belief and motivation. Every year I am able to use Robin's inspirational and positive approach to significant benefit in all aspects of my life. Who needs a life coach?' Sara Bobowicz, housewife and mother

'Robin Sieger's *Natural Born Winners* is a no-nonsense handbook on how you and I can overcome life's inevitable challenges and turn those experiences into powerful tools for managing change within corporations large and small. It's a read so dense in useful information that it takes two or three passes to fully appreciate. I've put his lessons to work at my company and the results have been phenomenal. I can't wait for his next work.' Matthew C. Barr, president, Carolina Color Corporation

'I picked up *Natural Born Winners* at a time in my life when every door seemed to be closed to me and life was one long journey filled with one disappointment after another. Robin Sieger has written an inspiring book which is for everybody who has seen their dreams slip away because they were afraid of failing. This is a book that will stay with me because it has become a constant friend and companion – not a condescending one, but rather one of those friends who holds your hand and just walks by your side while you reach your goals . . . all of them.' Hanadi Ei Diri, journalist, Lebanon

'Everyone looks at a winner with envy. Here is a book with the answers to make YOU a winner. Winners are NOT bred. Winners are well read. Here are the answers to make others envy you. Read them. Study them. And take them to the bank.' Jeffrey Gitomer, author of *The Sales Bible* and *The Patterson Principles of Selling*

'I thoroughly enjoyed *Natural Born Winners*. Robin Sieger has written a wonderfully inspiring book; he has the ability to give you a clear understanding of the secret ingredient common to entrepreneurs. I am sure it will give you a unique insight of what it takes to create personal success in life.' Peter Orton, chairman, HIT Entertainment PLC

'Once in a while, a book comes along that simplifies the seemingly endless parade of tomes dedicated to self-analysis. Robin Sieger astutely points out the discrepancies between how parents actively provide constant encouragement to their offspring in their earliest years, only to revert to a series of comments as they approach and enter their teenage years which serve only to undermine their self-confidence. *Natural Born Winners* reminds us all of the very real power of a positive frame of mind when matched to genuine aspirations and goals. I have been fortunate enough to have witnessed Sieger's prowess as a motivational speaker and heartily recommend *Natural Born Winners* as a reminder to us all of how we should conduct ourselves if we want to achieve our own goals and help others achieve theirs.' Nigel Gaymond, president, Gaymond International

'Whether I am negotiating a path through the world of business or weaving a route up a treacherous mountain, following the clear principles of *Natural Born Winners* hasn't let me down yet.' Neil Laughton, entrepreneur and explorer

'You know how people reading an engrossing book say "I couldn't put it down"? Well, I put down Robin's book all the time. In fact, it took me forever to finish it. The reason is that virtually every paragraph he writes gave me something to stop and think about. *Natural Born Winners*, enlighteningly practical, appealingly self-deprecating, and thoughtfully funny earns the highest praise I can offer. I couldn't read it fast.' Earl Pommerantz, writer and producer, Los Angeles

NATURAL BORN
WINNERS

Robin Sieger

arrow books

Published by Arrow Books in 2004

5 7 9 10 8 6 4

First published in the United Kingdom by
Random House Business Books in 1999

Arrow Books
Random House Group Ltd
20 Vauxhall Bridge Road, London, SW1V 2SA

Random House Australia (Pty) Limited
20 Alfred Street, Milsons Point, Sydney, New South Wales 2061, Australia

Random House New Zealand Limited
18 Poland Road, Glenfield
Auckland 10, New Zealand

Random House (Pty) Limited
Isle of Houghton, Corner of Boundary Road & Carse O'Gowrie,
Houghton 2198, South Africa

The Random House Group Limited Reg. No. 954009

www.randomhouse.co.uk

A CIP catalogue record for this book is avilable from the British Library

Typeset by SX Composing DTP, Rayleigh, Essex
Printed and bound in the United Kingdom by
Mackays of Chatham plc, Chatham, Kent

ISBN 9780099476672 (from January 2007)
ISBN 0099476673

To my father
Dr A. E. Sieger
Who taught me to love, to laugh, and to play golf,
in that order.

To Emily
Dream BIG!
Inspire others by
your actions.

All the best

Robin Sieger

CONTENTS

INTRODUCTION

Sometimes life can seem so unfair. You work hard, you do your best – but nothing seems to change. And yet there are others who, with the effortless ease of angels, always seem to get what they want. Why?

My father, a single-handed general practitioner in Glasgow, died at the age of fifty-two from a combination of overwork and stress. After a lifetime of dedication to his family and his patients, it seemed so unjust. And then, when I was only twenty-nine, and poised for the first time in my life to achieve a real degree of success, I was diagnosed with cancer. Talk about not getting a break.

Up until that point in my life I had vaguely hoped that I would be successful, that fate would deal me some luck and that I would enjoy a life of security and financial freedom. But curiously, although I knew my aspirations for the future required me to act, I didn't really believe it would make any difference whether I did or not. In other words, I felt my destiny was ultimately in somebody else's hands. So rather than going out to make the success I wanted happen, I was waiting for it to happen to me. The difference was crucial. In consequence, I lived at the time a life less than fully realised, suffering the silent rage of watching time pass me by, always ready to blame others or excuse myself – too willing to put my future on hold until something came along.

Even as a young boy I'd been the same. I'd wondered, like so many, what the future held for me. I'd wondered if I was going to fulfil my childhood dreams, whilst secretly believing I never would. That deep-bred belief in the inevitability of failure and disappointment was hard to shake. I went to an academic school believing I would fail: I was right. I even went to university believing I would fail – right again. These were truly self-fulfilling prophecies. But when occasionally I tried doing things at which I fundamentally believed I would succeed, the curious fact is that I did.

It was only after being diagnosed with cancer that I finally made the connection, that I got the wake-up call and in a moment of insight learned the lesson. That simple realisation was a life-changing experience for me, and one that has ultimately led to this book being written. It wasn't complicated or grandiose; I didn't unlock the secret of the universe, or discover a simple one-step method to instant happiness. But I did understand why winners win.

Over the next few years I read and studied everything I could and spoke to those whose experiences I could learn from. I distilled the recurring principles into a form I could make clear, simple, and put in to immediate effect. I understood that knowledge alone is not power; it needs to be properly applied for it to be truly powerful.

I began to use my knowledge and live my life in a more focused, positive manner, and the transformation was as dramatic as it was immediate and tangible. The anxiety and stress I had experienced in the past were replaced with strong feelings of confidence and peacefulness. I felt genuinely in step with life, or as I expressed it to a friend: 'at last the shoes fit perfectly'. My future was no longer a maze of uncertainties to be avoided but rather a journey of experiences to be embraced and enjoyed. I was happy.

As I reaped the personal and material benefits of my new philosophy I became full of enthusiasm for communicating it to others and helping them achieve success. I distilled the system into a two-day course that I called Natural Born Winners. Initially I ran the courses locally for free. Today the business has grown as I intended into one that develops the potential of individuals and organisations in the creation of success. We apply the Natural Born Winners philosophy in training courses on leadership, change management, customer care and team work – in fact on all areas of business and life where the outcome will be directly affected more by how we *think* than by how we *work*.

I now lecture at conferences internationally, and I recognise that the components of success are universal, timeless and constant – and have little to do with its apparent trappings. Success is no more a matter of luck than winning is simply about coming first or happiness about having lots of money. We all recognise and understand the paradox that you can be rich and still be poor; that you can enjoy huge status and yet still be miserable.

Successful people and businesses are winners on the inside. Success is an internal feeling with external manifestations. It wasn't that in my researches I had discovered anything new, but it was that I had discovered it for myself. As I have sometimes joked, life comes without an instruction manual – and yet we are born with the innate abilities to overcome its challenges. The closest we have to a manual is to be located within ourselves. We've just forgotten it's there.

I have written this book in order to share with you knowledge that is timeless and constant, and to introduce you to a practical, easy to apply programme that will develop your winning potential.

I haven't climbed Mount Everest or won an Olympic gold, but my journey to understanding has been every bit as demanding. I have experienced the frustrations of complacency and the anxiety of an uncertain future. Whatever frustrations you have experienced, be assured that I know where you're coming from.

Whoever you are, whatever your circumstances, this book is for you. I don't think of it as a self-help book. I regard it as more of a help-yourself book. Take from it those lessons that make sense and that you feel able to apply, and grow into the winner you were born to be. You can make a difference to your life if you apply the knowledge with understanding to create the future you want. It's rarely easy: you will need to stay the course with perseverance, commitment and determination. But you can do it.

I dearly wish I had known and understood as a young man the things I now know to be true. It's too easy to convince ourselves that we can't achieve the goals we set ourselves, that we cannot realise our dreams. It is my deepest wish that I may help you believe this: you can. Because I know that when you believe you can, you will.

1

Success

SUCCESS IS NOT A
PLACE OR A
DESTINATION. IT IS
NOT LARGE OR SMALL,
EXPENSIVE OR CHEAP.
IT IS A FEELING THAT
COMES FROM
ACHIEVING WHAT WE
SET OUT TO DO

Everybody's a self-made man; but only the successful ones are ever willing to admit it.

Anon.

What success means is not universal. Studies of people who have attained nearly identical achievements in the workplace, for example, find great variation in their level of satisfaction, with some considering themselves tremendously successful and others considering themselves average or even failures.

Maasen, G. and Landsheer, J. 2000. "Peer perceived Social Competance and Academic Achievement of Low-Level Educated Young Adolescents" *Social Behaviour and Personality*, vol. 28, pp. 29–40

SUCCESS

I was sitting with a group of fellow comedians in Los Angeles, all of them – like me – struggling hopefuls on the comedy circuit. I had taken myself there to learn all I could in a year by working in the most competitive comedy market in the world. It was 1985 and comedy was the new rock 'n' roll: success meant wealth, fame, and the ability to jump the queue at fancy restaurants, plus the obligatory fast cars, beautiful women, and a mansion in Beverly Hills. Such were the rewards we dreamed of, the Holy Grail we all sought.

I had been there for about six months and had slowly worked my way up the club circuit. No one was paying me yet, but at least I was working at weekends and there was always the possibility of being discovered – a possibility we all clung to. Of course, hardly anyone ever *was* discovered, so the usual thing after a show was for a bunch of us aspiring stars to head for a late-night bar or diner where we would while away the hours before making our way home, like wise sages critically dissecting the relative merits of rival comedians. So on this particular occasion, there I was at an all-night deli with a group of other comics, engaged in our favourite topic, when I began to notice that, almost without thinking, we were habitually dividing the comedians under discussion into two distinct categories: those who were doing even worse than us, we considered to have some talent, but were unlikely ever to make it to the big time. Those who were more successful than us, on the other hand, we mainly referred to as being 'lucky'.

Luck, we felt, was the determining factor in success: luck, which might – or might not – at any time touch one of us, in whatever guise. We all hoped that we had what it took to get to the top and we all hoped that luck would single us out. But we were wrong to look at success in this way. In fact the ones who *did* make it, never just hoped – they believed. That was the difference between us. That was the difference between their success and our relative failure. We hoped – they believed.

Since that early morning, I have been through a number of extraordinary experiences, which have forever changed my view of myself and my potential. And many times subsequently in business and in client meetings, I've heard people express endless variations of those conversations I had back in 1985 in Los Angeles.

> Success is not a matter of luck. Luck is a matter of random chance, while success is a matter of design

So if success is a matter of design, where's the blueprint?

The answer to that question has to begin with some understanding of what success means. If I were to ask you what you really want out of life, what would you tell me?

Money, fame, and freedom, or just to be loved perhaps, at the personal level.

But does having money make you successful? Surely not, or lottery winners, bank robbers and the heirs of great estates would automatically be considered great successes. What about fame? History demonstrates that fame is no guarantee of success or happiness; nor is personal freedom; and as for love, many people who are loved still feel they are unsuccessful.

Success is a matter of luck. If you want proof ask any failure

Earl Wilson (1907–1987)

I believe that the answer lies elsewhere, that success is best defined as the realisation of your goals, both personal and professional. Wealth, fame and many other trappings are simply by-products created by the achievement of those goals.

> Success is the realisation of our goals

Ask a successful person what they want out of life and the answer won't be vague or sweeping: they will give you a clear definition of what success will look like to them, a clearly defined goal that they've reached, or are still heading for. But that goal won't be a specific sum of money in the bank or a state of general happiness. It will be a very specific objective, the realisation of which will create the desired satisfaction.

This ability to clearly define a goal is part of what makes winners succeed. Winners have the same opportunities and disappointments as you and me. But they don't let setbacks reinforce a poor self-image; they see them as opportunities in disguise, as chances to bolster their resolve to succeed. What distinguishes long-term winners is the way they think, and their attitude. And those are the only two things in life that everyone has absolute control over.

> Success is not a matter of luck – it's a matter of design. Winners don't get more opportunities – they create more opportunities

Whatever dream you have for your future is within the realms of the achievable, provided it is within the realms of the possible. But the attainment of your goal will not be the result of reading a book (even this one) in the hope that it may reveal a hidden code or the framework for a get-rich-quick scheme. If you truly want your life to take the direction of success and happiness, you need to make a real commitment, create an unquenchable self-belief, feel a passion for what you are aiming for, and never, ever take your eye off your goal.

That man is a success who has lived well, laughed often and loved much.

Robert Louis Stevenson (1850–1894)

Luck doesn't come into it. The way you think does. Your attitude does.

Your success is your responsibility. It isn't anyone else's. When I first started my own business, getting an appointment with a prospective client was on a scale of difficulty somewhere between virtually impossible and forget it. I had no track record, and most companies either believed personal development training was a waste of time or had a preferred supplier with whom they were quite content. So when at last a prospective client asked me to make a formal proposal for a team-building programme, it was all I could do to stop myself from singing a one-man version of the *Hallelujah Chorus*. The only problem was that although I knew my methodology could easily be incorporated into a team-building event, I had little experience of team-building, and I wasn't sure how an effective team-building course was constructed. Then a friend put me in contact with a former military instructor he knew.

The fellow had served in the UK's elite military unit the 22nd Special Air Service Regiment. In my opinion he was wonderfully qualified to give lessons in team-building; what I learned from him and his colleagues was a revelation. At the core of the SAS's beliefs are: powerful self-belief, total commitment and a strong sense of personal responsibility.

The instructors I met at Hereford told me that the recruits who fail the regiment's physically punishing selection course ultimately fail themselves, either because they haven't prepared, or more simply because they choose to quit. 'You only fail when you quit' was a recurring theme amongst the men I met.

> ### You only fail when you quit

Those who pass selection, they said, suffer no less pain than the rest: their lungs burn as much, their feet are as sore, their muscles as strained. The difference is that those who pass find deep within themselves the determination to take one more step. They don't blame others, or look to a generous instructor in the hope he'll turn a blind eye, or seek excuses for failure. They have prepared, they are committed and they taken responsibility for their own success.

Some people make things happen, some watch things happen, and some wonder what happened.

Anon.

I also learned that by the third day of the selection process, long before it gets serious, the instructors can pick out those who will later pass. What they perceive can also be seen in the broader context. We have all met people with a special something – a charisma, self-confidence or some other indefinable quality – that marks them out as individuals bound for the top, people who attract others through their personality, who make everything seem worthwhile. These individuals have the feel of Natural Born Winners, and we can pick them out as easily as the SAS instructors pick out those who will pass selection.

What they all have in common is a very clear idea of where they are going, a plan that will get them there, and an unshakeable belief that they will succeed – strengths that we have already experienced, but that most of us have forgotten how to access and use. As our life experience has shaped both our self-image and our attitude to the world, we have too often learned to hope for the best while expecting the worst. But the good news is we all started life as Natural Born Winners, and, if we really want to, we can reconnect with the winner within.

CHANCE OR DESIGN?

Just as success is your responsibility and not a question of luck, chance also plays almost no part in your path to success. What does play a part is your perception of chance, and your readiness to use it to your advantage.

> It is only when you focus on realising a goal that you will perceive chance events as opportunities

Let's take a simple case that we can all identify with. You decide that you would like a short holiday in a warm climate. What do you do first?

You choose where you want to go and when. This is a clearly defined goal. Of course, you could just leave it to chance and jump in the car when the fancy takes you, without any thought of destination, but then you might end up spending the whole day debating whether to turn right or left at the first set of crossroads.

Luck is what happens when preparation meets opportunity.

Seneca the Elder (c. 55 BC–39 AD),

So you've planned when and where you're going; now you plan how. You work out a route, you buy maps, devise back-up plans, budget costs. You may take a chance on finding accommodation when you get there, to give yourself added flexibility, but you'll probably research all the places within your budget. In effect, you leave little or nothing to chance before you go. And it's precisely because you've done all this careful planning that you're now able to be flexible. Here's an example. You're driving along a pre-planned route and whilst feeling hungry you come across a sign for a restaurant down a country lane. Now, simply because you're en route to a planned destination, you're able to take advantage of the opportunity the local restaurant provides.

It is only when we have a clearly defined objective that we are able to take advantage of apparently random chances, because it is only then that we recognise the opportunity they offer. Put it another way: if you go through life looking for the lucky break without knowing exactly what you want to achieve in the long-term, then it's an odds-on certainty that you won't be able to recognise opportunities when you come across them.

Opportunities pass, they don't pause.

Anon.

I was eighteen when I hitchhiked by myself around Europe. During my six-week adventure I was often the recipient of great kindness. In Italy, a driver who had been behaving very oddly suddenly stopped and ordered me out of his car, serves me right for wearing my sister's ill-fitting kilt I suppose. It was about 10 p.m., dark and I felt very alone as I stood by the side of the main highway to Milan. No one was going to stop, so I walked across a ploughed field towards a light in the distance, and soon emerged through some shrubbery into a small village where people were sitting at long tables eating and drinking. I was immediately made welcome as food and drink was put in front of me. No one spoke any English and I spoke no Italian, but I do remember having a wonderful time. At the end of the evening a bed was found for me in a construction workers' dormitory and the next morning I awoke to find a simple breakfast laid out by my bedside. As I walked out of the village, many locals from the previous evening bade me farewell. On another occasion I was ill and was offered a lift from the doctor who wrote out my prescription. Throughout my trip I had many chance encounters – from which I benefitted. Where the chance encounters were threatening or, as on one occasion, even dangerous, I was able to avoid trouble by immediately recognising the situation – and taking the appropriate action. I soon realised that the experiences I had were in themselves neither simply 'good' (lucky) nor 'bad' (unlucky). What mattered was my ability to put each of them into the context of the whole trip. When opportunities arose, I would seize them and use them to my advantage, while threats were avoided at all costs. Both types of response were a matter of personal perspective.

> It's not chance itself that counts: it's what we make of it that matters

SELF-IMAGE

In his classic book of 1960, *Psycho-Cybernetics*, Maxwell Maltz describes his experiences as a Californian plastic surgeon treating people who wanted to improve their appearance. He tells the story of a beautiful woman intent on having a small blemish removed; she found it unsightly and consequently felt very unattractive. Realising that she was unlikely to listen to reason, he agreed to perform a corrective procedure. He happened to notice, meanwhile, that the woman's boyfriend, a short, unattractive man, had an ugly mole on his face. But when he mentioned that he could correct it, the man looked confused and said, 'There's nothing wrong with my appearance.'

> The you you see is the you you'll be.

This man's powerful image of himself as attractive affected the way he acted, the way he conducted business and – crucially – the way he thought about himself. It made him feel good about who he was. His girlfriend was the opposite. In spite of her beauty she had no real confidence in her looks, and the blemish became so magnified in her mind that it reinforced her inner conviction that she was fundamentally unattractive.

Take the example of a child learning to walk. On average, he will fall over about 240 times before succeeding. But the child never gives up. It's almost as if nature were saying to him, 'Get up don't quit, you can do it, get up, try again.'

What happens is that the fallen child picks himself up and, using the feedback information learned and stored forever in the brain, automatically corrects his mental image of the walking process. His abilities to learn, to acquire and to achieve are innate, and they are formidable. However many falls the child takes, his self-image is unwaveringly that of being able to walk. He doesn't get disheartened; he doesn't think of himself as a failure when he meets a setback; he subconsciously learns from his mistakes.

> The quality of our self-image – positive or negative – is central to our potential success

By adulthood, this innate conviction of inner potential has atrophied in most people. But the interesting thing here is that *successful* individuals always tend to have a strong self-image; they too believe without any doubt at all that they can reach their goals. These individuals accept that the process of falling over, of making mistakes, is part of the progress they are making towards their objective, and that it is in no way a reflection on who they are. This ability to accept that failure is not an expression of your being, but part of the process, is an essential ingredient of success.

A study in America showed that 96 per cent of four-year-olds had high self-esteem and a strong self-image. These children believed they had the world at their feet; they could become astronauts, ballerinas, pirates, cowboys, pilots – whatever they wanted. Their typical fantasy games showed how clearly they were able to visualise these dreams. The shocking part of the study was that by the time they reached eighteen less than 5 per cent had a good self-image. Along the way they had been told: 'You can't sing, you're clumsy, hey, stupid! Who do you think you are? You'll never be a success.'

As we grow older, our self-image is moulded increasingly by external influences, whether it be a teacher telling us we're incapable of learning, a parent insisting we're clumsy, or even a friend who, with the best intentions, implies repeatedly that our cooking is hopeless. Such comments are collected and stored in the subconscious. They become a template of who we now believe we are, erasing our original self-image and replacing it with a false sense of identity.

The problem is that if you have a poor self-image, you will always be looking for evidence to reflect or confirm it. If you believe you can't cook and you find yourself in a situation where you have to, you just know that something is going to go wrong. The minute it does, your first response is, 'I've always known I can't cook' – perfectly in tune with your current self-image.

If you think you can or think you can't, you're usually right.

Henry Ford (1863–1947)

How much, by contrast, is possible with a strong self-image? I remember asking the former SAS instructor in Hereford what he thought was the greatest thing the regiment had ever done. He offered me several alternatives: their successful Iranian Embassy rescue, their achievements in the Falklands and Gulf Wars. I disagreed with all of these. In my view, I told him, the greatest thing the regiment ever did was to call itself the *Special* Air Service. Consequently, it thinks of itself as special and, more importantly, its enemies think of it as special too. This sense of specialness is intensified by the rigours of the selection process, and the continuous references by SAS instructors to the regiment's stellar history, which reinforces the idea that its members are part of a unique elite. Given an image this strong at the core of its operations, it is easy to imagine the confidence instilled in every individual.

It's the same with children. They grow to the age of four being told they are *special* too – and you know what, they believe it!

DESTINY

> Your life is not predestined, it is not written in the stars.

When people talk of destiny they frequently do so in quasi-mystical terms, implying a predestination in which the unfolding of the moment of success is ordained by unseen forces. Many successful figures of the twentieth century have also had a sense of destiny, though not one that was necessarily preordained.

The self-belief, the identification of a goal and the commitment and perseverance that lead to its realisation are sometimes spoken of in terms of 'destiny'. When, as a twenty-two-year-old, my golfing hero Seve Ballesteros won the British Open in 1979, he said the win was his 'destiny'. Like virtually every great sportsman and woman who has reached the top, he always had the absolute conviction that, come what may, he would one day get there.

Whatever you can do, or dream you can do, begin it. Boldness has genius, power and magic in it.

Johann Wolfgang von Goethe (1749–1832)

What many call 'destiny' is, I believe, the result of a very clearly visualised goal that has become the driving force in an individual's pursuit of success. I can't prove it, but I doubt there is a single World or Olympic champion who has not from childhood seen themselves one day standing on the top of the podium. I'm willing to concede that when people with a great natural talent win a particular event, they may sometimes be justified in attributing their success to good fortune and to finding form on the day; but scratch deeper, and you will find someone who has dreamt big and unconsciously put into place the seeds of their own success. They might call it 'fate' or 'destiny', but I think George Bernard Shaw knew better. 'People are always blaming their circumstances for what they are,' he wrote. 'I don't believe in circumstances. The people who get on in this world are the people who get up and look for the circumstances they want, and, if they can't find them, make them.'

It is our actions here and now that determine our future experiences.

These people determined to make things happen. I do not believe the future exists in an inescapable form. Our destinies are for the most part determined by the goals we set. Do you dream big, and hope it will happen? Or have you stopped dreaming so as to avoid disappointment?

To be wronged is nothing unless you continue to remember it.

Confucius (c. 551–479 BC)

When something goes wrong, so many people express their disappointment in comments such as, 'I knew that was going to happen.' And they'll speak with the same conviction of being *generally* unlucky, or clumsy, or unsuccessful – 'Why does it always happen to me?' The heart of their argument is that events in their lives demonstrate time and again that they are unlucky, have always been unlucky, and expect to remain so.

But the reality is that they have created a powerful belief in their own misfortune, and anything that happens to them serves to reinforce that belief. They store the experience in their subconscious, thus confirming their poor self-image. When, on the other hand, they enjoy good fortune, it is at odds with the 'unsuccessful' person they believe themselves to be, so that they simply dismiss it, thereby avoiding any conflict of self-image or any chance of shifting their deeply held core beliefs.

Plenty of people carry around with them the negative labels they have been taught. I've known an accomplished pilot who still believed deep down that he was uncoordinated and clumsy; attractive people who believed they were ugly; smart people who believed they were dumb. The young child has few labels, yet they too were learnt, and normally they are powerfully self-affirming. How many little boys were told by their mothers that they were brave because they didn't cry when they hurt themselves? Or little girls going to a first party that they were the prettiest little princesses? A child's self-image is created by feedback from the world around it, which is almost invariably positive and supportive.

But for many of us as we grow, that image fades and is replaced with new feedback, which is frequently negative and destructive. We're not the bravest boy or the prettiest girl, we are not as clever as we believed and our sporting abilities were not as world class as we had imagined. Our image of ourselves from childhood fades, and is replaced with negative beliefs that we use unwittingly to define ourselves.

> Change your self-image and you change yourself

If you think of yourself as clumsy, unsuccessful, ugly, unmusical – or whatever it is that you hold at the core of your self-image – your subconscious will sabotage or deliberately filter away any information that might contradict, or conflict with, your self-image. And it's the quality of that self-image that will determine how you will deal with obstacles on your path to success.

SETBACKS

We all inevitably suffer setbacks of one kind and another – that's what happens in life. But if we have a clear belief in, and commitment to the realisation of our success, often through adversity, if we are able to create a 'never-quit' personal philosophy, then we will see setbacks simply as obstacles to overcome, as challenges to our ingenuity. If we don't have these strengths, on the other hand, setbacks will be the tools that destroy our self-belief. They will become, in our minds, insurmountable problems that wreck our confidence in our ability to complete the task we have undertaken. We will use them as excuses to explain away failure: it's not our fault that we are not making progress.

If you have a negative attitude you will identify even minor setbacks as major obstacles and blow them out of all proportion. The result generally slows you down, leads to a great deal of time and energy being wasted, and takes you further away from your goal.

> Opportunity is missed by most people because it is dressed in overalls and looks like work.
>
> *Thomas Edison (1847–1931)*

Successful people in contrast put setbacks into perspective. They recognise that things beyond their control – for example bank interest rates, the weather, the reliability of associates – will often go wrong. What they do is accept it, resolve it, and get on with the task in hand.

Too many of us use setbacks as an excuse for having failed to achieve what we set out to do, and we distance ourselves from the failure, by saying: 'I was just too exhausted', 'They never called me back', 'I was just so unlucky'. There is never a shortage of setbacks, which, for one reason or another, allow us to justify giving up. But in reality, what we've done is quit. What we didn't have, to use a boxing analogy, is the ability to take a standing count, clear our heads, refocus and get on with the task we set out to achieve.

Whatever the circumstances.

COMMITMENT

Riding through setbacks towards your goal requires more than just a strong self-belief and a clearly defined objective. It takes commitment. Commitment is similar to determination, except that while determination may be an emotion of the moment, commitment is a steely underlying will that endures through all changes in circumstance. A massive factor in success, it is an intangible ingredient to which much lip-service is paid, and which, dangerously, is often mistaken for enthusiasm.

What's the difference? Commitment and enthusiasm are both wonderful qualities often found at the heart of success, but enthusiasm is something we can fake to those around us, simply by appearing positive and energetic.

You may be able to fool others for a short time, and you may even be able to delude yourself for a while, but in the end, commitment is either present or not; you cannot fake it. An example makes this clear. We have all at some time, with the noblest of intentions, determined to change that ever-present aspect of our lives that we feel can always be improved on: our weight and/or our fitness. We buy a book, we join a gym, do whatever we feel is required to get us started. And we all know, I guess, what usually happens next.

Good thoughts are no better than good dreams if you don't follow through.

Ralph Waldo Emerson (1803–1882)

There won't be any problems this time. It's really going to work, it's going to be different from all the other times. You are determined, you've splashed out on a fancy machine with some clever name like the calorie-counter-o-matic and bought enough fresh fruit and vegetables to worry an environmentalist. You've even joined a gym and invested in an ergonomically-approved pair of branded sweat-pants. You are *very* committed – or at least you think you are. In fact you are probably just full of enthusiasm and hope.

> There is no in between – you can no more be slightly committed than you can be slightly pregnant

You get up early and prepare your bowl of bran and oatmeal with gusto, follow with half a grapefruit and wash it down with a cup of rosehip tea. Later, at the gym, you go through the prescribed exercises and return home feeling very pleased with yourself. But as the days go by, the results are slow to materialise and you start to feel your enthusiasm waning. Only slightly, at the beginning, but as the weeks pass your commitment all but disappears until finally you really can't be bothered any more and so the diet or fitness regime joins the list of previous failed attempts. And with each failed attempt you know deep down that the likelihood of a future attempt failing has increased, creating a failure habit.

Ultimately we fail on these occasions because, no matter how much we may protest at the notion, we *expected* to fail. What we took for real commitment was no more than desire. Someone once said that gratitude is the shortest-lived emotion. Perhaps – but I believe enthusiasm comes a close second. Enthusiasm, which in team events can generate so much energy and excitement, is in the last analysis no substitute for commitment.

Imagine you've lost your arm in an accident and arrive at the hospital to find two doctors waiting on stand-by, one very enthusiastic, the other very committed – which one would you like to sew your arm back on?

When you commit to an objective, you have to do so with 100 per cent belief that you are going to realise it. The commitment switch has two positions: on and off. There is no in-between. And it is the passionate commitment in the minds of successful achievers that stops them from quitting; that keeps them believing and persevering no matter how hard the going gets, because they know that in the end they're going to get there.

Examine the depth of your commitment to something or someone you absolutely believe in – your family, a loved one – and imagine what you would be prepared to do to help them in time of adversity. It's a powerful feeling. And it's the level of feeling you need to create in the process of making yourself truly committed to success.

> ## Your life is up to you. Life provides the canvas: you do the painting.
>
> *Anon*

COURAGE

Along with real commitment, success requires courage. We often associate courage with bravery, and though I have no doubt they are closely related, bravery has perhaps more to do with extraordinary, even impulse-driven, personal responses to exceptional situations where life itself may be at stake. Our own capacity for bravery is something that may never in our lives be tested. Courage, on the other hand, is a quality that we all possess and need to use daily: and when we do so, we start to make remarkable progress.

Courage is the ability to do something that, for whatever reason, we instinctively fear. It can be something we experience every day – fear of ridicule, fear of failure, fear of change – or a host of other things from which we naturally draw back. We draw back to feel safe. And although what we then achieve is not what we had wished, it is at least something we are comfortable and familiar with.

But when we remain with the familiar, change becomes harder and harder; we become more risk-averse, and we reinforce the barriers that make us content to leave things just the way they are. Success only begins to happen when individuals with self-belief and the passion to succeed are prepared to overcome their fears and learn from the experience.

Only those who dare to fail greatly can ever achieve greatly.

Robert F. Kennedy (1925–1968)

It's rather like someone on the flying trapeze who won't let go, won't make that essential first move in the acrobatic feat he's about to perform, because as long as he hangs on he is safe. Eventually he gets tired and runs out of momentum, and ends up dangling, going nowhere. In time, he gives up, falls and lands in the safety net. By contrast, the artist who becomes a star is the one who, though afraid to let go, believes it can be done because the worst that can happen is that she'll land in the safety-net and learn from her mistake.

Similarly, in order to get to where we want to go, we often need to find the courage to let go of where we are, by facing our fears and learning from our mistakes. And the fuel that fires our courage – to start up in business, to explore an unmapped land, or simply to learn a new skill – is the passionate belief that success is not only achievable, but in the end guaranteed.

For success-oriented people it is not the fear of failure that holds them back, but the fear of living their lives less fully and regretting the things they never attempted. Indeed fear of failure may be the very thing that drives them on. At the end of our lives we do not regret the things at which we failed: we regret the things we wished for but never attempted.

Let's suppose you're starting your own business. You get a fax line installed in your bedroom, have stationery printed, and flyers distributed locally, and send 100 letters to prospective clients. Nothing happens. So you decide the next step is to set up face-to-face meetings; the dreaded cold call. The problem is that, try as you might, you can't do it – you just want to quit every time you're halfway through dialling the number.

Even if you do get through its odds on you'll be so nervous that you'll ramble on pointlessly, apologise for calling, and fail to secure a meeting. Why? Because the fear of rejection, of being patronised makes us pull back from a commitment to trying. Our imagined sense of failure is greater than our imagined sense of success.

Strangely, the courage we require to overcome this is not so different from the courage of our personal heroes. It demands perseverance and the setting of achievable objectives; entertaining no doubts in their future success; focusing clearly on those objectives; and committing ourselves to not quitting under any circumstances, to take action and go for it.

When it comes to the first step, take action and go for it. When it comes to the much-feared cold call, commit yourself to making five every day, then twenty, then forty, until you *deconstruct* the limiting belief that you have created. You will then perceive the cold call as part of the process, without which that process will not function. The main fear that has to be overcome in life is fear of failure itself. Failure is something that happens, a lesson to be learned from: it is not evidence that you are always going to fail.

Jack Nicklaus, the greatest golfer of the modern era, told one young professional embarking on his career that he never forgot that he had failed a lot more frequently than he had succeeded.

When you fail, learn from the experience: don't identify with the experience

We must learn to see failure as part of the learning curve: when we fail, it just means that we are not doing it – whatever it may be – right. Surveys of successful salespeople in America, of the consistently highest performers, show that one thing they have in common is that they only started to get appointments and sell their products after the sixth or seventh approach. These salespeople were not lucky; they were committed to the task; accepted failure as part of the process; and were courageous enough to have overcome the fear of rejection.

How do you find that courage? The answer is simple. Focus so clearly on your objective that you see and understand every step in the direction of its completion as an essential part of the process, leading to your success.

BELIEF

I mentioned earlier in this chapter the importance of self-image. The image you have of yourself is the person that people meet. We are all too aware when someone is being a 'phoney' – all the image-consulting and window-dressing in the world will fail to disguise a poor self-image for long.

Your beliefs at a personal level represent your core values. They determine how you see yourself, who you are and what you believe you can achieve. They dictate how you approach problems, respond to situations, conduct all aspects of your behaviour.

These core beliefs are rather like the DNA that carries your genetic code: no matter from which cell in your body you take the sample the information contained within it is exactly the same. And it's this information that provides the blueprint for your physical make-up.

Do the thing you fear, and the death of fear is certain.

Ralph Waldo Emerson (1803–1882)

Similarly, your core beliefs have a consistency that informs every aspect of your behaviour. So if you believe absolutely that you will succeed, almost anything becomes possible. A strong belief-system can enable individuals to achieve seemingly impossible aims, allowing them to overcome fear, ridicule, hardship and even pain: a strong belief-system can enable them to dissociate themselves at a personal level from difficulties or setbacks.

But a strong belief-system will not overcome vague life-goals such as: 'I hope to start my own business but I'm not sure what it'll be,' or 'I hope, if I'm lucky, to get a pay rise,' or 'I'm waiting to see what happens.'

If your train's on the wrong track, every station you come to is the wrong station.

Bernard Malamud (1914–1986)

Our core beliefs deeply influence our ability to succeed. When they are strong and positive they enable us to believe that the goal we have set out to realise already exists in the future, and that we are capable of achieving it. Believe with 100 per cent certainty that success is achievable and that failures along the way are no more than life offering you a learning experience, and you will create an inner confidence that needs no image-consulting or window-dressing. The you that people meet is a person with a very clear idea of where he or she is going in life, and people will notice that you have a special something that makes you stand out. Your core beliefs are not only the foundation of your actions – they permeate your thinking.

They can because they believe they can

Virgil (c. 70–19 BC)

How you think impacts directly on how you behave, and how you behave impacts on how you perform, and how you perform impacts what you achieve.

FEAR

However strong our commitment, courage and belief, it will always help us to understand our fear. Fear in itself is not a bad thing: it can draw our attention to a future challenge and serve as a wake-up call to the fact that action needs to be taken. The fear response is a basic instinct that keeps us alert to serious danger; but in our daily encounters there are less dangerous situations to which we react with variations on the theme of fear – feelings that range from a general uneasiness, through anxiety, panic and on to debilitating stress. Our bodies physically manifest the emotional response to being afraid: fear causes our heart to race, palms to sweat and stomach to get butterflies. It is these emotional responses to our fear that hold us back, because we naturally seek to avoid them.

Two men look through prison bars; one sees mud, the other stars.

Frederick Langbridge (1849–1923)

I believe that most fears are based on events that only occur in our imagination. The things we tend to fear are not those that have happened or are happening, but those that we believe could and will happen. We will examine this in more detail later. But think for a moment now about the time and energy you put into creating fear-inducing negative scenarios, and then imagine how different it would be if that same time and energy were spent thinking about successful outcomes.

The happiness of your life depends upon the quality of your thoughts.

Marcus Antonius (86–161 AD)

There is a story of a prisoner in a Chinese gaol in the 1930s who, a week after his trial, had been sentenced to death. His guards kept a close eye on him, to stop him depriving them of his public execution. But whenever they visited his cell they were amazed to find him cheerful, writing letters, singing, and ready to joke with them. They thought he was crazy, and as the days passed his behaviour never varied. On the day of his execution, the guards brought him his last meal. One, unable to bear it any longer, asked the prisoner how he could be so cheerful, knowing he was so soon to die. He answered, 'I am alive now. The future has yet to happen, so now I'll enjoy being alive now.'

Live in the now

Ask yourself, then, 'What you are afraid of and why?' I'm not taking about phobias, which often have their roots in childhood traumas, though these too, when faced can be overcome. I'm talking about those 'events' in the future that you believe are going to happen. The more you believe that they're inevitable, the more strongly they exist in your mind as *real* future events. And more often than not, once you believe it strongly enough, they will happen.

Fear traps us in our past. It is extraordinary how often with friends and colleagues we enjoy reminiscing about 'the good old days', when everything was more secure. Of course it was: the past is always more secure – it can't change. And when we do think back, we tend in any case to select happy experiences. But we don't seem to laugh and joke so much about the future and what it may hold, or speculate on why we delay making positive changes in our personal and professional lives. Perhaps it's because we're adhering to the procrastinator's motto, 'Next week I'll get it done' – and in the meantime we'll stay where we are, because compared with what we imagine awaits us, the past is a pretty safe place to be.

> Recognise the illusory nature of the fear, and let it go. Vividly imagine a successful outcome and replace the negative expectation with that – and focus all your efforts on making that new future a reality.

> Remember that no matter how real whatever you fear will happen in the future appears to be, it has *in fact* not happened

MOTIVATION

There is an old joke which tells the story of a man returning home one night after the late shift. He decided to take a short-cut home by way of the cemetery. It was raining hard and the wind was blowing, and suddenly in the pitch dark he fell into a freshly dug grave. He landed heavily, and now he was wet, covered in mud and angry at his misfortune. However, he was fit and very determined to get out, so he tried to jump; then when that proved useless he took a run-up –

but again without luck, so now he thought he'd try climbing. The soil was clay-based, though, and he couldn't get a hold, so finally he decided to curl up into a ball in a corner, try and stay warm, and call for help in the morning. He settled down accordingly, and drifted off to sleep.

As it happened, some twenty minutes later, another fellow from the same shift, also cutting through the cemetery, stumbled into the same freshly dug grave. Now this fellow had had a few drinks, and was short and rather unfit. All the same, he tried first to jump out, then to climb. Without success, for a full fifteen minutes, he put all his effort into escaping his current predicament, but to no avail. Exhausted, he was standing there in the dark and the rain when suddenly from the corner of the grave he heard a voice, 'You'll never get out of here,' it said ominously.

But he did. As soon as he heard the voice he jumped straight up and out.

Our motivation is an internal engine, one that we control, although frequently it is external experience which acts as the trigger to finally push us into action.

> Passion and commitment are like oxygen and petrol in the combustion engine – they require the spark of motivation to create power

Motivators are powerful catalysts inspiring us into action; whether basic ones like hunger or dramatic ones like the voice from the grave. Apart from hunger our motivators at the basic level are survival and shelter. Our hunger motivates us to find food, our need for warmth motivates us to find shelter, and so on. Great motivators understand the importance of this internal drive. In the sporting world there have been coaching legends who have harnessed the powerful force of a motivated team: these individuals have known that passion and commitment are internal experiences for each individual player – experiences which, unlike interest or attention, cannot be faked.

But you can no more motivate yourself by saying, 'I've got to get motivated,' than you can get fit by simply joining a gym and then waiting for something to happen. Instead you have to identify the triggers in your life, then go out there, use them and make them work for you, just like the machines in the gym.

At one conference I spoke at, a young fellow came up to me and asked me how I could motivate *him*. I said that short of pulling a gun on him, I didn't have a clue. The purpose of my talk, I explained, had been to share with the audience my experiences and thoughts, and in the process to inform, engage and hopefully inspire them to act, and to believe in their ability to make real changes. I hoped the talk would spark them into action. The commitment and passion must come from within – and that, I said, was *his* responsibility.

REMEMBER

- You must define exactly what success means to you – otherwise it will be impossible to achieve
- See it clearly in your mind – power-fully imagined
- Revisit the image – as often as you can

2

YOU THE HERO

HEROES ARE PEOPLE
WE ADMIRE, WHO
DEMONSTRATE
QUALITIES WE RESPECT

Nurture your mind with great thoughts; to believe in the heroic makes heroes.

Benjamin Disraeli (1804–1881)

Feeling there is meaning in your life is eight times more likely to produce satisfaction than a high income.

King, L. and C. Napa, 1998. 'What Makes A Life Good', *Journal of Personality and Social Psychology*, vol. 75, pp. 156–65

YOU'RE UNIQUE

As children we are so often told of the uniqueness of snowflakes, that no two are exactly the same. We are told the same of our fingerprints, of our voices, of our DNA; so we can take it for certain that each and every one of us is a unique individual. Yet despite our understanding that we are all individuals, we habitually compare ourselves with others.

> Never in the history of the world has somebody like you existed. Don't waste the opportunity

We use them as yardsticks against which to measure our success. How often have you read in a newspaper of somebody who's achieved great things, then quickly checked that they *are* actually older than you, thereby giving yourself at least some temporary reassurance that you may yet equal their success.

But comparing yourself with other people is a meaningless exercise because you will never know what *their* motivators are, what drives *them*, what abilities *they* have that are unique to them. There will always be skills that others have that you wish you had; equally *you* have skills that other people wish they had. We often, wrongly, assume that skills must be musical, artistic or intellectual to be of any great value, while in reality we all have marvellous gifts, integral parts of our make-up, that we continually overlook, such as compassion, patience, humour, understanding, kindness or good communication – all of them strong tools that we can use to help us achieve future success.

In the end, continually comparing yourself with others can only adversely affect your self-image, your self-belief and your ability to achieve. The main person whose gifts you should examine to see if they are being fully exploited is you.

> Our self-image and our habits tend to go together. Change one, and you automatically change the other.
>
> *Maxwell Maltz* (1899–1975)

We are all unique as individuals, but what I think makes us unique as a species is our ability to bring about change in ourselves through the exercise of conscious thought.

Scientists now believe that 50 per cent of personality and ability is inherited through our genes – which means that 50 per cent of it is not. And that 50 per cent it is up to us to create and develop. What would you most like to change if you could? Of course, we must accept that there are things we were born with that no amount of positive thinking is going to change – our height, our eye and skin colour, and so on. But we can change the way we think about them, and that is a powerful quality. So often I come across people who say, 'Oh, I'm nobody special.' The reality is that you are – but if you do not believe it, it's a certainty that no one else will.

> Everyone is somebody special

Think of a child in infancy. She receives an enormous amount of praise and unconditional love, she's told how special she is – positive reinforcing messages to the developing mind. But as we get older this input slows down. One particularly significant factor here is that we learn to conform, to fit in. We don't want to stand out from the crowd when we go out to play, we don't want to be different from other children; we become nobody special. So the conforming process is something we teach ourselves in childhood. It's a time that determines the development of our self-image, and later in life we seek to stay within the boundaries of that image because it is safe. We forget that we really do have the ability to change, any day we want to.

Try this exercise right now: think of a person whom you can describe in one word. You might choose 'funny', 'humble', 'thoughtless', 'gentle', 'selfish'. Now think of one positive word to describe one aspect of yourself that you're proud of. This is the first step towards identifying yourself – not only who you are, but who you want to become. Small details in self-awareness make a big difference.

INDIVIDUALITY

Your individuality is your sense of who you are. If you have a clear image of who you are, you will not allow yourself to be defined by labels. Don't define yourself by the job you do, the house you live in, the car you drive, or the clothes you wear. You are *not* the sum total of these things. It is in themselves that successful people believe. Their potential to succeed is dependent not on status or labels but on a quiet confidence that they have it in themselves to get where they want to go.

> Death is not the greatest loss in life. The greatest loss in life is what dies inside us while we live.
>
> *Norman Cousins* (1915–1990)

A bishop was lying on his deathbed. He reflected to his wife, 'When I was a young man I was determined to change the world, so I went around telling everyone how they should live and what they should do. But,' he went on, 'it didn't seem to make any difference because no one really listened to me. So I decided I would change my family instead. But, to my dismay, even they didn't pay any attention or make the changes I wanted from them.'

He paused and sighed. 'Only now,' he said, 'in the last years of my life, have I recognised that the only person upon whom I could exert any real influence was me. If I wanted to change the world, I should have begun with myself.'

If you want to change the world, change yourself first

Whatever your ambitions in life, the road to success and achievement is a road you walk alone. Yes, you can travel alongside others on the path you tread – your teammates, family, or colleagues – but ultimately, it's a solo journey. No one else can take the steps for you.

Similarly, if you want to be a winner, whatever your field of endeavour, it is you and you alone who must make the effort to get there. It is through the exploitation of your natural gifts that your goal will be realised. Nobody can lose weight for you, nobody can get fit for you – you have to accept personal responsibility. To be an individual does not mean being isolated – it's about identifying who you are and choosing what you want to be. This gives you the potential for success that you had never dreamt possible.

When I first started researching personal development, I thought that claims of guaranteed success were far-fetched because they seemed to offer too much too easily – instant wealth, instant satisfaction. In fact the methodologies offered none of those things. What they revealed was this: you alone determine what it is you want to achieve, and your power to do so lies in believing it's possible, and in taking action. Only you can determine what *your* success is. Making the commitment to achieving it doesn't guarantee that success. But not making it does guarantee failure.

People are always blaming their circumstances for what they are. I don't believe in circumstances. The people who get on in this world are the people who get up and look for the circumstances they want and, if they can't find them, make them.

George Bernard Shaw (1856–1950)

Recognise opportunity

The road to success begins when we seize an opportunity and work hard to turn that opportunity into personal achievement. But the first step is to recognise the opportunity for what it is, and that is simply a matter of perception.

There was an old priest who lived in a valley. For 40 years he looked after all the people who lived in his parish. He conducted the baptisms and the funerals, married the young couples, comforted the sick and the lonely. All that time he was the perfect example of a good and holy person. Then one day it began to rain, and it rained and rained in biblical proportions until after twenty days of non-stop downpour the water was so high that the old priest was forced to get up on to the chapel roof. There he sat shivering when a man came along in a rowing-boat and said, 'Father, quick, get in and I will take you to the high ground.'

The priest looked at him and answered, 'For 40 years I've done everything God expected of me and, I hope, maybe a little more. I've done the baptisms and the funerals, I've comforted the sick and the lonely, I only ever take one week's holiday a year. And when I have that week's holiday, do you know what I do? I go to an orphanage and I help the cook. I have great faith in God because this is the God that I serve, so you can go with your boat and I will stay. My God will save me.'

The man in the boat left. Two more days passed and the rains reached such a level that the old priest was clinging to the very top of the steeple as the waters swirled around him. Then a helicopter arrived and the pilot called to him, 'Father, quick, we'll send down a winch. Put the harness around you and we'll take you to safety.'

The old priest replied, 'No, no', and again he gave his speech about his life's work and his faith in God. So the helicopter left, and some hours later the priest was swept away and drowned.

Being a good man, he went straight to heaven. Furious at his fate, he arrived there in a very bad mood. He was squelching angrily through heaven when all of a sudden he came upon God. And an astonished God looked at him and said, 'Father Macdonald! What a surprise!'

At which the priest stared at Him and said, 'Oh! A surprise, is it? For 40 years I did everything you ever asked of me and more, and in my moment of greatest need you let me drown.'

God stared back at him, bewildered: 'You drowned? I can't believe that – I'm sure I sent you a boat and a helicopter.'

I skate to where I think the puck will be.

Wayne Gretzsky (1961–)

The reality is that the boats and helicopters of opportunity are always there – we just have to recognise them. That comes down to a matter of perception and expectation, and we can only really do it when we have set ourselves an objective. It's only then that these apparently random occurrences, which we would normally have been blind to, will be evident as the opportunities they are. Almost every event creates an opportunity. There are exceptions, of course – personal tragedies such as bereavement. But we should try to accept these as facts of life, events over which we have no control, and allow ourselves to grieve. What we mustn't do is use them as excuses for doing nothing.

An immigrant to the United Kingdom – or indeed to any First World country – is statistically four times as likely to become a self-made millionaire as someone born there. Is it because immigrants are four times luckier? We've already seen that there is no such thing as pure luck, so the answer is definitely no.

> Whatever your life circumstances, your starting-point is not an indicator of where you are capable of going

Are they four times harder working? Again no – there are only so many hours in the day. Maybe they are four-times cleverer then? But that's not it either. Many self-made millionaires left school without formal qualifications what they have in common is that they are four times more likely to recognise an opportunity, because they're looking for it.

There is never a wrong time to do the right thing.

Anon.

The essential point is this: your frame of mind is crucially important in determining how open you are to identifying good breaks that come your way. If you are in a negative frame of mind or have a poor self-image, if you don't believe you will be successful, then you are unlikely to recognise opportunities, and nothing is worse than wasted opportunities.

> Success has very little to do with background. It has a great deal more to do with self-belief, the ability to recognise an opportunity and the courage to act

Indeed, I believe that the real tragedy in life is not failing to reach our goals, but not having goals to aim for. I sometimes hear people say, 'I don't get breaks, I'm just not a lucky person.' What's happened is that they've closed their minds to the chances around them; like the old priest, they're blind to the boats and helicopters.

So don't wait to take those opportunities; don't put it off until tomorrow; don't end up at the age of eighty-five wishing you had done all the things that you have the chance to accomplish now.

Save worry and anxiety for the major upsets in life. Today make a conscious effort to see something positive in every situation.

Anon.

YOUR PAST DOES NOT DETERMINE YOUR FUTURE

You have no doubt occasionally met people who say, 'It's just the way it is,' 'That's my lot,' or 'Nothing good ever happens to me'. It has been said that if you do what you've always done, you'll get what you've always got. Our subconscious determines how we think, how we respond and how we act. Believing that you've always been a failure only works if you hold firmly to that belief. But you *can* break out of that conviction, if you choose to do so. I said earlier that anything you believe to be true about yourself is understood on a subconscious level. Furthermore, your subconscious mind cannot distinguish fact from fiction, and will continually seek to reinforce whatever the dominant subconscious image you have of yourself by encouraging actions that confirm it, or inhibiting actions that would contradict it. You only have to look at the effects of hypnosis to know this is true.

> Change is the one constant in our lives; to resist change is ultimately to sow the seeds of personal failure

We must accept that as change occurs we too must change. Yet often when people are offered a promotion, the new responsibility and expectation create anxiety. When asked to change, they resist. They are being asked to do something which, judging from past experiences, they don't believe they are capable of doing. Rather like the beautiful caged bird – all its life imprisoned, fed and watered by its owner. One day the owner dies, and a neighbour comes along, opens the cage door and says to the bird, 'OK, now have your freedom.'

But the bird stands in the doorway of the cage, looks all around and thinks to itself, 'I'll just stay here, because this is the world I know, and for all its limitations I'm safe here.' What the bird doesn't realise is that outside the cage is a world to be explored, a wonderful world of opportunities.

> The past has gone; we can't change it. Let it go

How many of us have gone for a job interview convinced that we're terrible at interviews, recalling on the way there, all the memories of being turned down? This rehashing of old failures unconsciously creates an emotional response in the form of stress, which manifests itself in headaches, irritability, and a 101 other ways. The more stressed we become, the more likely we are to create a self-fulfilling prophecy by giving a poor account of ourselves at the interview, so that when the bad news comes through we can say with complete conviction, 'I knew I'd never get that job!'

Good people are good because they've come to wisdom through failure. We get very little wisdom from success, you know.

William Saroyan (1908–1981)

Let me share another story with you. I played golf for my university. Now, I have a unique record there because before my final game I had played 21 matches and I'd lost 21. Just before my last game as a student I remember thinking, 'I'd like one victory before I leave, to regain in the eyes of my team a small measure of dignity.'

The team captain told me my opponent had a handicap of twelve – my handicap at the time was seven – so I thought I had a good chance. I teed up against him as the last match out. He hit a wonderful drive and, surprisingly, I followed with a rather good drive of my own. We both made par at the first and the second. At the third hole he went one up and stayed one up until I got it back at the ninth. By the tenth hole we were both only two over par, playing extraordinarily good golf. We got to the fourteenth, where I levelled the game. At the fifteenth I went one up, we tied the sixteenth.

As we walked towards the seventeenth hole I said to this fellow, 'Where do you play your golf?' He mentioned a championship golf course. I was amazed, and when I asked him how that had come about, he told me he used to play for Cambridge University first team. To play for Cambridge University's first team you need a very low handicap: certainly a lot better than twelve. Puzzled, I asked him what his handicap was. 'Two,' he said.

You see it appears that my shortsighted captain had read two as twelve (in fact he had had too much wine at lunchtime). The minute I discovered this man's next handicap, my confidence left me with a speed I had never imagined possible, and was replaced by all the memories of losing.

Needless to say, I didn't disappoint my subconscious mind. I lost the seventeenth and ultimately the eighteenth hole – my 100 per cent record for defeat intact. As long as I'd believed I could win, I'd had a winning manner about me – the way I walked, thought and played, hey I was good!. But the minute I believed I had no chance, everything changed.

> Being a champion means thinking like a champion. Winners win because they visualise the rewards of success; losers lose because they visualise the penalties of failure

A professor of business management who was in charge of the department's office expenditure once told me how one day he'd noticed that his secretary had bought twelve pairs of scissors. When he asked her why, she replied, 'Because my predecessor always did.' It turned out that in the days before computers, when speeches and notes were being written, a lot of cutting and pasting went on. No one had realised that as times changed, they ought to change with them.

If you have a bad or unproductive habit ask yourself the question, 'Why am I doing this?' If you don't like the answer make a definite commitment to change that procedure. There is always another way of doing something. At a more general level, recognise that the learned patterns of behaviour you employ are shaping your future. If you want those patterns to continue, leave them as they are. But if you're not happy with them, then you have the choice and the ability to start the process of change right now. Complacency, indifference, and procrastination are your main enemies.

DREAM BIG

Everything begins with a dream, so dream big. But don't expect to get there in a single leap (leave that to Superman). We are all familiar with the Confucian proverb: 'Even the longest journey begins with one small step.' So commit yourself to the journey you are about to make and take that first step. Because if you don't, the journey will never begin and the dream will stay just that. A dream that isn't followed by action remains an idle wish. A dream that generates action can change the world. Furthermore, you are capable of creating any future scenario you want, so don't limit yourself to small dreams and small ambitions. If you aim big and come up short you are still going to be a lot further along than you had previously thought possible.

The fountain of contentment must spring up in the mind. He who has so little knowledge of human nature as to seek happiness by changing anything but his own disposition will waste his life in fruitless efforts and multiply the grief which he purposes to remove.

Samuel Johnson (1709–1784)

I am inspired by the example of Terry Fox, a young Canadian, who was diagnosed with bone cancer and had to have his leg removed in order to prevent the spread of the disease. Moved by the suffering of other cancer patients, he determined to run across Canada to raise money for research. With the support of the Canadian Cancer Society, Terry began training for the 'Marathon of Hope'. On 12 April 1980, in a farewell gesture, he dipped his artificial leg in the Atlantic Ocean and left St John's, Newfoundland, with a target of 26 miles a day. Capturing the imagination of a nation, his run was closely followed in the media.

Terry's dream was to raise $100,000. 'I guess that one of the most important things I've learned is that nothing is ever completely bad. Even cancer. It made me a better person. It has given me courage and a sense of purpose that I never had before. But you don't have to do like I did – wait until you lose a leg or get some awful disease – before you take the time to find out what kind of stuff you're really made of. You can start now. Anybody can.'

On the outskirts of Thunder Bay, Ontario, 143 days and 3,339 miles later, Terry stopped running. The cancer had spread to his lungs. But by 1 February 1981, when the Terry Fox Marathon of Hope Fund totalled $24.17 million, his dream of raising $1 for every person in Canada had been realised. On 28 June, one month short of his 23rd birthday, Terry Fox died. Every September since then, at points all around the world, his legacy has been celebrated with the Terry Fox Run. The foundation has raised over $180 million; in the Rockies a mountain has been named after him, and there is a huge memorial outside Thunder Bay. Terry Fox inspired millions.

Three days after his death a journalist wrote, 'Terry Fox's race is over. In fact, he never finished the course; none of us ever do. What is important is the running. What is important is to set goals. What is important is not to quit, not ever. What is important is to run well and honestly, with as much human grace as possible – not forgetting, too, to take joy in the running, to laugh at life's absurdities as well as weep at its cruelties.'

Terry Fox dreamt big. All winners dream big. The kind of dream I'm talking about, of course, is the conscious kind, the kind that we control. All of us have daydreamed, consciously created a fantasy situation in our minds. We should daydream more, because it's the activity that underpins the visualisation techniques that are an important aspect of realising our goals, and that we shall discuss in more detail later.

It is also very important, when you have a dream, not to share it with people I think of as dream-stealers, people who undermine your ambitions, who say, 'You can't do that. You're bound to fail!' It's vital to share your dreams only with people who fully believe in you and your ambitions, who will be catalysts, encouraging you at those inevitable times when you feel disheartened and negative.

Dreams work for individuals, and they work for business. Under Jack Welch, the chairman and chief executive officer of General Electric, the American company became one of the biggest in the world. He has always had a great belief in setting ambitious goals – dreaming big, having ambitious targets, he called it stretch: 'Stretch in its simplest form says "nothing is impossible", and the setting of stretch targets inspires people and catches their imagination. Stretch means using dreams to set . . . targets with no real idea of how to get there, and as soon as we become sure we can do it, it is time for another stretch.'

The subconscious will always move towards the image you hold of yourself – which includes your goals. If you are convinced that you will realise your goals, you will create the conditions which assist your progress. Equally if you are convinced that something bad is going to happen, you will create the circumstances that allow you to become discouraged and lose confidence when some unexpected challenge is encountered. You will see such occurrences as the failures you had anticipated – and identify with them. People who habitually fail have a powerful failure mentality. They have encoded into their subconscious the belief that they will not succeed and unconsciously follow a pattern of behaviour that fits in with that belief. Those who succeed, by contrast, have a powerful success mentality. Usually without realising it, they have encoded in their subconscious the image of future success.

> Dream big, shine brightly and dare to fail

So it's important, when you are setting goals for the future – when you dream of the victories that lie ahead – that you think positively and dream big.

BECOME YOUR OWN COACH

Why do the best sports stars in the world have coaches? If they are the best in the world in their fields, what can anybody possibly teach them! The point is, of course, that like many peak performers, they understand that a coach serves many functions: to encourage them at times when they are feeling down, to help them look for strategies that will give them the competitive edge that they have found in the past and that they know they can recreate in the future, to help put them in the right frame of mind – a winning frame of mind. But just as important is the coach's talent for praising, for reinforcing the positive images of victory that allow them to stay at the top of their chosen professions.

> There are high spots in all of our lives and most of them have come about through encouragement from someone else.
>
> *George M Adams* (1837–1920)

Parents recognise that encouragement is vital when you set out on the path towards becoming a Natural Born Winner. It is essential that you keep in your subconscious the positive images, expressions and statements that relate to you as a success. Your parents in effect become your coaches and one of the qualities of coaches is that they are enthusiastic. Enthusiasm is infectious; we can receive it and pass it on. If you genuinely believe in your goal, enthusiasm will come automatically, because belief and commitment demand it. If you run into difficulties recall not your failures but your past successes, and hold these memories in your mind. Reaffirm your future goal. Get into the habit of thinking positively, praising yourself when you do something well. Reaffirm the experience by saying to yourself, 'Well done! Good!'

Affirmations are expressions that allow you to reinforce an already positive self-image. They act as triggers to your subconscious, helping to strengthen the image of the person you are seeking to become. The French pharmacist and psychotherapist Émile Coué, who lived at the turn of the twentieth century, used to tell his patients to say out loud: 'Every day in every way I'm getting better and better.' When he compared these patients post-operatively with other patients who used no such affirmation, he found that his patients did indeed recover much faster than the others.

Think of some affirmations that will work for you. Whatever you choose, keep them simple. They must always be in the first person and relate to a future state that you are moving towards, for instance: 'I am becoming healthier now,' 'I am actively moving towards my goal now,' 'I am becoming calmer every day.' Say them to yourself throughout the day, out loud. And don't worry about feeling self-conscious – it will be worth it, because it *will* work. You can often see athletes before a critical moment getting themselves fully prepared. They go through a ritual of settling their nerves and telling themselves: ' I can do this,' 'I'm ready,' 'This is the one.' Watch their lips; watch the results.

The artist is nothing without the gift, but the gift is nothing without work.

Émile Zola (1840–1902)

Imagine you are coaching your best friend, someone you love dearly, who depends on you entirely to help her achieve an ambition. How would you go about it? Think about it, and then apply that same approach to yourself. If you are planning to achieve certain changes in your life, don't be afraid to seek assistance. Look to people you admire, who have done what *you* are trying to do. Ask them how they did it, what pitfalls to watch out for, about the disappointments that they encountered and how they overcame them. Even at the highest levels, advice can help.

After winning a number of PGA tour events, Nick Faldo, then an extremely gifted young professional golfer, approached the golf teacher David Leadbetter to ask him to help him develop a completely new swing that would stand up to the pressures of world-class golf and bring him major championships. It was a very brave thing to do – people thought he was crazy, committing professional suicide – but he believed that if he was going to achieve his aim he had no choice, and he set about rebuilding his swing. He went on to win three British Opens and three US Masters titles.

If you go through life vaguely hoping for the best but preparing for the worst, the worst is what you'll get. If, on the other hand, you are *determined* to achieve the best, then it is up to you to give your-self every chance to do exactly that. Work out the plan you want to follow, become your own coach, encourage yourself constantly, and when you come up against difficulties, ask for help. This is simply all you have to do. You will be amazed how many people will gladly help you on your journey.

OVERCOME THE FAILURE HABIT

When I was a young man, and as far back as my schooldays, I always believed I would fail, that I wouldn't pass crucial exams. This was caused by a number of factors that I now recognise. I allowed myself to be easily discouraged when I made a mistake. I identified myself with failure; I didn't see myself as simply lacking knowledge or understanding. In fact I thought I was just not academic, not smart in the traditional sense (in other words I thought I was plain dumb). One thing I was certain of was that I wouldn't get into university. When I was sixteen, six weeks before the 'O' level chemistry exam, our science teacher went through the register one name at a time, predicting who would get a grade A or a grade B. When he came to me, he just said, 'You're going to fail; you're wasting your time. You're not going to pass anything.'

I remember being enraged by this, by his insensitivity, by his bul-lying satisfaction – and if his intention was to galvanise me into doing something, it certainly worked. Off I went to the bookshop and bought myself *Teach Yourself Chemistry* and the course books for years 1, 2 and 3 – I was currently on year 4. Then I spent two weeks, seven days a week, ten hours a day and more, putting myself through the entire course, from the basic structure of the atom up to the fourth-year syllabus work. I took the 'O' level, and not only did I pass but I scored a grade B, which meant I had achieved 60–69 per cent. Even more importantly, I truly believed that I could go to university after all. The news generated some looks of astonishment amongst the teachers, but two years later I went to university.

Up until that point in my life, all the things at which I had believed I would fail, I *had* failed. I had predicted, in very clear terms to myself months if not years before, that failure was inevitable; often I would tell others that I didn't believe something I hoped for would materialise. Accordingly, it never did. Amazingly I still didn't make the connection.

What I had mistaken as some vague sense of personal destiny became in fact a self-fulfilling prophecy. I had programmed my sub-conscious to expect failure; in fact, it demanded failure. The wonderful workings of the brain enabled it to fulfil my negative expectations. Every time a failure that I had predicted became reality, it reinforced my belief that it was my lot in life to fail, and that there was nothing I could do about it. It wasn't until the life-changing wake-up call of being diagnosed with cancer that I determined never again to allow myself to think like this. I now knew that I was fully responsible for the way I thought. My habit of believing failure to be inevitable had been the very cause of my failure. I had been safely ensconced in a prison of my own making; getting out of my comfort zone had been just too damned hard, too scary. The changes I had wanted to make, I hadn't wanted to be responsible for – I'd wanted them to just happen. I'd wanted to wake up and find my world OK.

Believing failure to be inevitable is often the very cause of failure

Personal failure is not about losing, it's about repeating a pattern of behaviour that you feel comfortable with. If I asked you how you feel when you fail, what would you reply? Would you make an excuse, or maybe mutter a resigned acceptance? How do you justify your failures? Many people just make a joke of it, as though they don't really care. But believe me, it is important that you do care because, once you care enough, that will become your trigger. It will be the catalyst that enables you to start making real changes. Your past failures are events that happened in the past. They are not what you are about; they are not labels that you should stick to yourself and forever identify with. They are just things that happened – learn the lesson.

> # Each problem that I solved became a rule which served afterwards to solve other problems.
>
> *René Descartes* (1596–1650)

Any change we make in our lives has to follow a natural order of progression. It's very much like learning to run. We have to learn to crawl, to stand, and to walk first; there are no short cuts. And if we determine that we are going to succeed, we must learn how to break the failure habits we have spent a lifetime learning.

How do we do this?

Identify the point at which your personal failure mechanism starts to kick in. Normally it starts with saying something negative or visualising the inevitability of defeat. Memories of previous failures start to weaken your determination.

Stop using negative talk – 'I can't', 'I won't', 'I'm not able to.' Speak positively when you refer to your future goals, when you speak about yourself, *and* about other people. And remember that just as habits are learned, so they can be unlearned.

FIND THE HERO WITHIN

What is a hero? I think a hero is someone who does something that he or she is naturally afraid to do – someone who does a thing that requires courage. Heroes are people we admire for their actions, and whose qualities represent to us an ideal. To many young boys their father is a hero. He is perceived as brave, fearless and strong – all qualities that young boys aspire to develop. And the interesting thing is that children *believe* that they can be just as heroic. It's not just demonstrated by the kinds of games they play. Remember that 96 per cent of four-year-olds have high self-esteem; they believe they can do anything they want to. But by the time they are eighteen, fewer than 5 per cent still have that high self-esteem. So what happened to these children to make them lose their sense of self-worth and potential? Research has shown that on average parents speak to, rebuke or instruct their children negatively 90 per cent of the time. Given that the average twelve-year-old is estimated to have received over 100,000 negative sound bites during his or her life, it's easy to see how inadvertently a child's self-image can suffer. Although no parent knowingly seeks to undermine their child's confidence or self-esteem, the demands made on parents often mean that they are unable to sit down and explain their actions to the child. But the effects of praise versus blame culture – or the positive versus negative approach – can be clearly seen in terms of the developing self-image. Then add to this the negative messages coming from school and peer groups: 'You can't do this', 'You can't sing,' 'You're stupid.' Any child, whether he is particularly impressionable or averagely resilient, will, if he hears enough criticisms about himself, end up believing them. And the image of himself that forms in his mind will be based on them.

But the amazing thing is that, despite all this, the memory of that potential, that self-belief, *remains within us*. I believe that within each of us there is the real person we were born to be, a dormant hero with whom we have lost contact. That hero had absolute conviction in his ability to succeed. And the success we're talking about isn't to do with winning bravery awards or getting medals for acts of courage on the battlefield – it's about being able to stand up every time you fall down, and to having the belief that no matter how often you fall down, you have the determination to get up one more time. As it was succinctly put to me whilst I was training for an endurance event: you only fail when you quit.

A winner is simply someone who gets up one more time than he fell down

It is very important that we reconnect with those positive self-images from our early childhood, because when we do we reinforce them at a subconscious level. So that every time we achieve something that we would naturally shy away from, we are forming a powerful positive memory, building a stronger self-belief, and further expanding the limits of our horizon.

Live as you will wish to have lived when you are dying.

Christian Furchtegott Gellert (1715–1769)

When I was lying in my hospital bed after my operation, awaiting the results of the various tests they were running, I started to imagine my funeral and, more specifically, the tributes my friends would be paying to me. I must admit that my imagination came up with some quite wonderful eulogies, expounding on my many extraordinary achievements (well at the time I thought they were – the folly of youth!). This got me thinking, later, that we should always design our lives back to front. Think of the things you would like to be said of you at the end of your life, think of the things you would like to have achieved, and no matter how exceptional they may be, go for them. Write an obituary you would be proud of, and set about making it happen now.

The thing about heroes is that in fact they are ordinary everyday people like you and me – they just do things that to us appear extraordinary. When we overcome the things in our lives that we are afraid of, that hold us back, we are performing acts of private courage by breaking through our firmly held limiting beliefs. And those acts of courage vastly improve our self-image along the way.

I have a godson called Finn. When he was four years old his father Tom and I took him for a picnic. We came to a small river that had to be crossed with the aid of stepping-stones, and because of Finn's age and lack of confidence, Tom picked him up and carried him. On the way back, Tom again carried him across. I hung about on the other side of the river and, for a joke, called to him, 'Finn, Finn, come and get me, I'm afraid of the water.' Finn turned to his father, expecting him to do something. Tom, though, playing along, pretended that he was in a hurry to get back to the car. 'We'll have to leave Robin behind,' he said, and walked off. Finn watched his father disappear, and then looked at me. 'Don't leave me, Finn,' I said. Suddenly his face became a mask of concentration – his two little hands formed into fists and he began to prepare himself to cross the river. He planted his foot on the first stepping-stone, at which point I ran across to stop him going any further. If a child of four, I realised then, could find within himself the resources to overcome what was probably a considerable fear in order to help somebody, then what greater power adults must possess when they face their fears and overcome them.

The actions of men are the best interpreters of their thoughts.

John Locke (1632–1704)

It's taking the first step that seems so hard. But take it, no matter how small, because it's that step that will start you on your journey to whatever goal you have set yourself. It's a short step. And only you can take it.

REMEMBER

- You are a unique individual – with greatness within you
- Until you take action – nothing will happen
- Do not be afraid

3

THE BIG
SECRET

THERE IS NO SECRET
RECIPE FOR SUCCESS –
IT'S RIGHT THERE IN
FRONT OF US

The only limit to our realisation of tomorrow will be our doubts of today.

Franklin D. Roosevelt (1882–1945)

Successful people spend at least fifteen minutes every day thinking about what they are doing and can do to improve their lives.

Sigmund, E., 1999. "Consciously Directing the Creative Process in Business", *Transactional Analysis Journal*, vol. 29, pp. 222–227

THE BIG SECRET

As a boy I read about alchemists who studied hard to turn lead into gold. They were probably the first people to seek the lazy man's way to riches – which I imagine is the title of some book somewhere. It's the type you see advertised in the backs of magazines and on the Internet with appealing titles such as *How to Make Money While You Sleep*, or *Ninety Days to Your First Million*. The only people who ever got rich from those adverts are the people who placed them.

No doubt many of us would love to discover a magic bullet; a recipe for success; a Holy Grail that after years of searching is found upon a mountain top and bestows upon its finder great happiness, joy and wealth.

Just think how happy you would be if you lost everything you have right now, and then got it back again.

Anon.

But after many years of meditating cross-legged deep in thought on a mountain top in Scotland (all right, a table top in London), I have finally discovered the big secret, and I can no longer keep it from the world. I am prepared for the first time to reveal what it is and I hope you are ready because it may come as a big shock: *there is no secret.* But don't be disappointed by this – don't slap your forehead in despair. All is not lost. Instead all is found.

I do believe there are some straightfoward principles that are common to those who have enjoyed and continue to enjoy success. The basic ingredients of success are neither complex nor obscure. They have always existed, they have not been invented, they have simply been discovered. I believe that successful individuals operate seven basic success principles, often without any awareness that this is what they are doing. Some, of course, emphasise one aspect much more than others – indeed, no two people ever use exactly the same combination. But, rather like different chefs cooking omelettes, though the taste and texture of the finished products may differ, they will all contain the same ingredients.

THE SEVEN PRINCIPLES FOR SUCCESS ARE:

1 A clear goal
2 A definite plan
3 Confidence
4 Purpose
5 No fear of failure
6 Commitment
7 Celebration

1. A clear goal

Both teams in a football match know that the object of their endeavours is to put the ball in the back of their opponent's net – in other words, to score goals. In life, too, success is most commonly realised by those who have clearly and concisely predetermined the exact nature of their goals. These individuals are very specific about what they are after.

You'll never hear them say anything as: vague as 'I'm going to start a business and make lots of money,' or 'I hope I play better today'. Such concepts are impossible for the brain to visualise and, since your brain thinks in images, it needs to visualise clearly what it is seeking to achieve. (See appendix – Brain.)

First say to yourself what you would be; and then do what you have to do.

Epictetus (*c.* 50–138 AD)

At the subconscious level too, a vague goal is very difficult, if not impossible, for the mind to visualise clearly, and therefore to focus on and to work towards.

Your goals may be extremely ambitious, but as long as they're realistic they're achievable.

Bill Gates's clear goal has been to bring personal computers within reach of every householder. Roger Bannister's goal was to break the four-minute mile. Edmund Hillary's was to reach the summit of Mount Everest. Mother Teresa's aim was simply to help the poor and dying abandoned by society. I don't know whether she ever dreamt that the Sisters of Charity would go on to become a worldwide organisation, but, be that as it may, her goal was very clearly defined.

Have you defined your goal?

To be blind is bad, but it is worse to have eyes and not to see.

Helen Keller (1880–1968)

Every goal starts out as a thought, as a daydream. But in the winning mind-set this goal, this image, becomes real, almost tangible – as though it really exists in the future. When you ask people to describe their perfect house, they can usually draw you an extraordinarily detailed picture. When you ask them to do the same with a car, you get a similar response. But when you ask most people about their life-goal or their perfect future they usually can't tell you so precisely – they haven't clearly defined to themselves what it is they wish to achieve.

I think your dream life is more important than a house or car.

Those rare individuals who, by the realisation of their goals in the twentieth century, transformed our lives, not only saw clearly what it was they wanted to achieve, they believed in its attainability. When you ask such people to define success, they usually talk in terms of achievement rather than monetary gain. Financial reward was for them a consequence of success rather than their main focus.

Whether it's simply to lose a few pounds or to make two extra sales calls a day, or to build up a business that will transform the world, clearly define to yourself whatever it is you wish to achieve.

2. Definite plan

> If you fail to plan, then you are planning to fail

Once you have clearly defined your goal, the next step is to plan exactly how you are going to get there. Furthermore, you need to have faith in the plan and your ability to execute it, particularly with ambitious goals, which may seem at the outset almost fanciful. You need a plan that you can believe in even if you don't yet have the evidence to support it. It need not be sophisticated or detailed, or even foolproof – it doesn't have to resemble the blueprints for the Space Shuttle – but what it does need to be is something that you can understand and that can give you a starting-point.

It is perfectly all right for your plans to change weekly or even daily, depending on how the situation alters. The best plans are infinitely flexible – if they don't work, change them, adapt them – as often as you need to. The truth is that if a plan is too inflexible and begins to fail, then the goal becomes an even more distant spot on the horizon. The individual's confidence in their ability to reach that goal is diminished, and morale slumps.

Build milestones into the plan as you pursue ambitious long-term goals: it is essential to have planned short-term indicators to check whether you are on course. Think of a sailor navigating the ocean or a pilot flying long distances: they have Way Points or Reporting Points every 20, 50 and 100 kilometres in some cases, just to confirm that they are on course. So it should be with your plan. Work out the designation.

When schemes are laid in advance, it is surprising how often circumstances fit in with them.

Sir William Osler (1849–1919)

Imagine you want to drive from Glasgow to London: you would make sure that you know the journey was progressing in the right direction by having directional indicators. When you pass by Carlisle, then Manchester and Birmingham, you know you are going in the right direction. With life goals, the same principle applies. If you have a long-term aim in mind, make sure you are on track by giving yourself many achievable short-term goals. Once one is in the bag, tick the box and move on to the next.

Eventually you will see these short-term goals accumulating to create your ultimate goal.

Give me a stock clerk with a goal and I'll give you a man who will make history. Give me a man with no goals and I'll give you a stock clerk.

J. C. Penney (1875–1971)

When people go shopping they often draw up a shopping list. They decide in advance what it is they want to buy, knowing that when they get to the shop, they can always take advantage of any special offers, even though they didn't figure on their list. But if you don't make a list, it's very easy to arrive home only to discover that you've forgotten something essential. Similarly, if you are going to have a dinner party, you plan who to invite and what they are going to eat. You may well use a recipe book for guidance; you may even decide in advance where your guests are going to sit. You don't leave any of these things to chance because you know they are all important for the success of the evening. Your life is infinitely more important than any dinner party – why do so many people leave it to chance and then feel surprised when it doesn't work out.

> Plan your life; don't leave it to chance

If you *don't* plan your personal and professional life goals, you will be subject to the vagaries of chance and it's quite likely that you'll end up somewhere you don't want to be.

In the pursuit of your personal goals you may, of course, be tempted to let someone else map out your route for you – but do this only if you want to end up making *their* journey.

Ultimately, you have to plan *your* journey yourself. And remember, when you are clear in your own mind about where you're going, it's best on the whole to keep your plan to yourself. Share it only with those who will support, encourage and most importantly believe in you.

Before you take action in pursuit of your dreams, ask yourself, 'Where's the plan?' If you haven't got one, get one.

3. Confidence

The word 'confidence' derives from the Latin *cum* (with) and *fides* (faith), meaning the faith in something or someone – in this case yourself – that grows from the assurance of positive past experience. It's different from arrogance – arrogance is the product of an over-inflated ego believing in itself without any evidence to substantiate that belief, and is frequently characteristic of an insecure or *un*confident person, who tend towards being unattractive personalities.

Imagine you've been rushed off to the casualty department of your local hospital. You've broken your nose, you're in great pain and your nose needs to be reset. Standing at the door are two doctors, both about the same age. One gives the impression of confidence and compassion, the other of arrogance and indifference. Who would you want to treat you? I don't know about you, but I'll go for confidence every time. Truly confident individuals and organisations are invariably humble: they have no need to boast of their successes because, having achieved in the past, they have that quiet inner knowledge that they can achieve again.

When you're setting an ambitious goal, confidence enables you to rise above the negative values of others, allows you to overcome endless setbacks – as well as ridicule, fear, hardship, pain and all the other hurdles you may encounter. The faith of confident individuals in their ultimate success is critical to the accomplishment of any endeavour. We only have to consider those many famous explorers and scientists whose belief in the achievability of an ambitious future objective was initially met with derision. Confidence inspires others; it is the key component of the leader.

The big question is, how do we acquire confidence? We can't go to the chemist and buy a bottle of it, sadly. However the continual achievement of small personal successes helps us to build it up – slowly but as surely as if we had swallowed a dose of a magic potion.

In this way our confidence is born not of wishful thinking but of authentic experience, both good and bad; the good reaffirms, and the bad is a lesson to be learned. Taking quiet pride in who you are and what you are achieving forms the bedrock upon which your confidence will be built.

The great pleasure in life is doing what people say you cannot do.

Walter Bagehot (1826–1877)

4. No fear of failure

The future doesn't exist. Or rather it exists only in our imaginations, though I am sure a few science fiction writers might disagree. But although the future doesn't yet exist in any tangible form, we frequently fear it because of its uncertainty. Those same imaginations which identify our goals will, in moments of self-doubt, create equally strong images of failure, something that we shy away from for fear that it will harm us. We tend to see failure as signalling the end of our hopes and wishes, but it need not be so. If instead we choose to see failure positively, it marks a new beginning. Think of the young infant learning to eat and to talk. She doesn't worry about the fact that most of her food ends up almost anywhere but in her mouth when she's feeding herself, nor is she bothered by any grammatical errors she may make when trying to ask her father for her teddy. She isn't influenced by peer group pressure. She is motivated by a natural success mechanism that helps her to achieve, to learn and to survive. She has no concept of failure, so she has no fear of it

Make the most of every failure. Fall forward.

Anon.

Fear of failure can stop you from even trying, but there really is no great shame in failing. As I said earlier, I believe the greatest shame is in never trying. The point is that no successful person ever associates himself with his failures: he regards them as opportunities to learn valuable lessons.

When you fail you will learn that no one else really noticed or cared as much as you did

Thomas Edison, a prolific inventor among whose many patents the light-bulb was arguably the most renowned, made over seven hundred attempts before finding the right material for the perfect filament. When he was asked how it felt to fail so many times, he replied, 'I haven't failed, I've just found seven hundred ways that didn't work.' He saw it in a positive light (forgive the pun!).

Neither our lives nor our careers are races to see who can get there first – they are journeys that produce an equal share of setbacks and of achievements. What matters is your ability to face your fears, to overcome them, and to realise that they only truly exist in your imagination. I'm not suggesting that you now take up cave-diving or bomb disposal as hobbies. Rather, pick one thing that you have always said no to in your life because you were afraid. It could be something as specific as learning to swim, or as general as fear of rejection – or even, fear of success.

Godlike genius? Godlike nothing – sticking to it is the genius.

Thomas Edison (1847–1931)

Examine exactly what it is that you are afraid of, and recognise that fear exists in your mind. The more you believe in your fear being real, the more it becomes your dominant mental image of the future, and the more likely it is to become a self-fulfilling prophecy. See your fears for what they are – merely false expectations that appear to be real – and smash them.

Pinned above the desk in my office is a quote: 'At the end of our lives we don't regret the things at which we failed – we regret the things we wished for but never attempted.'

So what are you waiting for?

5. Purpose

Purpose to me means having a deeper value behind your goals. It is about having a personal sense of meaning. When you set a goal for which you have no real purpose, and from which you will not gain any benefit, it is unlikely you will feel personally inspired to see it through to completion. On the other hand if the goal you set has a real purpose behind it, and you add a passion to that purpose, you create significance. And by significance I mean what happens when your inner sense of meaning engages with the world around you in a positive manner and to a positive effect.

Everyone needs purpose, it gives a sense of meaning to our actions without which we lose interest, grow bored and eventually give up. We need a clear purpose behind our goals, and we need to want them passionately, because when we marry passion to purpose, we have self-motivation. Have you identified your purpose? What lies behind the goal you seek? Keep asking yourself the same question, 'When I achieve my goal what will it give me?' Whatever answer you get, ask yourself again, 'What will *that* give me?' And to every answer repeat the question. When you can no longer answer, you will have found the purpose. I think you will be pleasantly surprised when you hear what it is.

> Our goals enable us to realise our purpose

I once embarked on a personal challenge to raise money for a charity by attempting to play the eight most extreme golf courses in the world in less than one calendar year.

This would include the highest, the lowest, hottest, coldest, most northern, most southern, the greatest, and the toughest. My goal was to complete the challenge, as by doing so I would benefit a charity I love and support. I doubt if I would have bothered otherwise, as it would involve 40 days travelling (and for someone who travels as much as I do that is no real incentive). My purpose came from knowing no one had ever completed such a feat before, and that I personally could make a difference in the lives of others.

The highest course in the world is La Paz Golf Club, in La Paz, Bolivia. I arrived and had to spend five days acclimatising to the altitude at 12,000 feet, though the course itself is situated at 10,650 feet. Getting used to the altitude was part of the planning; Neil my colleague in the venture was an experienced mountaineer, who had reached the summit of Mount Everest in 1998, so when he said we needed to acclimatise, there was no discussion.

Most days we would go for walk, and think about what we would eat that evening. The altitude surprised me as it was very easy to get out of breath, so playing a full round of golf, carrying clubs was going to be very tiring. There are thousands of street vendors in La Paz selling everything you could imagine, and then stuff you would never have imagined. One day I noticed a woman selling greeting cards at a very simple stall. I passed by in the morning and late in the evening and she was always there. On the third day I noticed a cardboard fruit storage box beside her, I glanced into it and saw a child wrapped up warmly and sleeping, very quickly I took a photograph, which I keep on my computer and have often shown at conferences, to explain exactly what I mean by purpose and passion.

What was this woman's purpose? I believe it was in caring for and providing for her child; and for her passion – well a mother's love for a child needs no explanation. In my experience, successful people always have a strong sense of purpose backed up by powerful passion.

Purpose and passion are the building blocks of personal motivation

Personal purpose has a side effect from the things we do for ourselves; it is often the case that our actions impact beyond our expectation, that we add to the value of an endeavour, that we touch or are touched by acts of kindness, compassion and helpfulness. In short we make a difference.

This feeling that our purpose has a wider value and serves others is, for me, at the heart of building our goals in our minds. For the musician it may be to share her music, for the builder to provide homes for people to live in, for the person seeking to lose weight it may be to live long and to make their family proud of them. Even the young man stacking shelves in a supermarket, though he may have no sense of it, is going to make life a little easier for someone else through his work. No matter what we do and what goals we aim for, creating a strong sense of benefit that goes beyond ourselves and into the lives of others, will help us find our purpose.

6. Commitment

Commitment is doing the thing you said you'd do long after your initial enthusiam to do it has evaporated. It gives us the ability to stick to our plan and our goal, yet it is the first thing that goes when we start to give up.

Why do we lack commitment? Why do people give up on a dream? I suspect that they've learned that the easiest person in the world to let down is themselves, and it is OK to quit because they have mastered the art of excusing themselves. They find it easy to let themselves down, because in the final analysis they don't care enough.

It is a curious thing that we will let ourselves down and not follow through on our good intentions, yet we rarely let someone else down so easily, even a stranger. Why? Is it because we feel a sense of responsibility, or that we don't want others thinking badly of us, or perhaps because we don't like people letting us down so we try not to hurt the feelings of others?

I once arranged to meet a friend at the British Open Golf Championship and we agreed to meet at the practice area at midday in front of the stand. On the day in question the weather forecast had not been promising – rain was predicted, and it arrived. I was working long, hard hours producing a television show at the time, and on that Saturday morning when I woke up the last thing I wanted to do was travel to the event, stand in the rain, and get wet, when I could watch it on television, in comfort. The only problem was I had no way of contacting my friend. I had no option but to go, it never crossed my mind that I could just not turn up. Had I been going on my own – no problem. But the idea of leaving someone waiting and standing in the rain – no way.

The quality of a person's life is in direct proportion to their commitment to excellence, regardless of their chosen field of endeavour.

Vince Lombardi (1913–1970)

So I duly got to the designated meeting place, and waited and waited. In fact I waited for an hour and a half and though it was raining only lightly, I was royally disappointed. Cold, wet and miserable is never a good feeling, but to be let down is a lot worse.

We met up in London some weeks later for a drink, and he explained that he'd been on a conference call that he just could not get away from. It sounded pretty convincing but then unfortunately his girlfriend arrived and while he was at the bar she unwittingly revealed that they had in fact been at the event, but at the appointed hour he had decided it was too far from the practice ground to meet up with me and given the weather, convinced himself that I probably wouldn't have been there anyway. We didn't fall out as friends, and I have dined out on the story many times since (in fact it gets better with age) but it clearly illustrates commitment in action, and the possible consequences of a lack of commitment.

You must be committed to the goal, the plan and to yourself. Don't let yourself down, because when you do, you take away a little more from being the person you want to be.

7. Celebration

It is very important to celebrate every successful goal as we move through life. It seems strange that we celebrate the success of children as they grow and in so doing, enable them to develop a strong self image; yet as adults we hardly ever to expect praise, and celebrations are largely reserved for birthdays and other holidays.

However, we witness tens of thousands of sports fans jumping for joy and yelling at the top of their voices when their team scores a goal or wins a match. The emotional journey one can take through a sport is powerful and the memories of certain events remain with us for the rest of our lives.

In November 2003 in Sydney, Australia, England won the Rugby World Cup. It was a fantastic result for the English. For four years they had set out with one goal – to win the 2003 Rugby World Championship. The last world championship to have gripped the nation so completely was 37 years earlier in 1966 when England won the football World Cup. Throughout the country the heartfelt support for the English rugby team was tangible, and they were the favourites – which brought its own pressures. Their game plan did not always go smoothly, and their route to the final was not the triumphant procession that had been anticipated. But they got there.

They got to the final and they played one of the most dramatic matches I have ever witnessed in any sport, culminating in the dying seconds of extra time, when the tension made watching almost unbearable, and the fly half, Jonny Wilkinson dropped a goal in the most exhilarating finish imaginable.

After they returned to England and a hero's welcome at the airport, it was announced that there would be an open top bus procession through the centre of London. On the day, over 800,000 people lined the streets to watch as they drove by – to applaud the team and catch a glimpse of the trophy and the players. People had travelled from all over the country to be there to celebrate. They took time off work, they took their children out of school. The cheering was deafening. Everyone had come to share in a moment of pure celebration.

> Celebrate success, learn from failure and live in the now

Why should we celebrate anything? Because celebrating makes us feel great, which is always a good thing. It creates a very strong emotional memory, so strong that when we remember the event the emotional memory returns. And it follows that the more of these events we experience through our own successes, and the more we celebrate them the more we build up a powerful self-image of high achievement, and the more closely we associate ourselves with future success.

So celebrate your successes no matter how small. It is a very powerful and important way to reinforce successful self-image and it feels good too.

PERSISTENCE

I used to think that maybe persistence was the eighth guiding principle. Now, though, I believe that it's the all-important common thread running through the seven principles of success.

Before you start your journey and determine exactly how you're going to get to where you want to go, ask yourself this: 'How badly do I want it? How badly do I really want this success?' Because you have to want it so badly that you can see it, smell it and feel it.

History is full of people who have shown great persistence. They are frequently the people we remember as heroes.

Press on. Nothing can take the place of persistence. Talent will not; the world is full of unsuccessful people with talent. Genius will not; unrewarded genius is almost a proverb. Education alone will not; the world is full of educated derelicts. Persistence and determination alone are omnipotent.

Calvin Coolidge (1872–1933)

All those years ago when I went off to Los Angeles to try my hand at comedy, I spent months going from club to club, trying to get a spot, trying to persuade TV companies to give me a chance to write for them, discovering first hand the harsh realities of life. Along the way I met Peter, a performer whose dream was to become a screenwriter. We became friends. I returned to England, and it was soon afterwards that I was diagnosed with Hodgkin's disease and spent some months in hospital before returning to work in British television. Peter and I stayed in touch via the odd letter and phone call, and over the years I would see him when I visited Los Angeles. He was a lovely guy, very joyful and full of self-belief but over the years he went into bad debt. He was getting older and one evening, in a moment of serious concern for his future and the major disappointments I felt sure lay ahead, I said, 'Peter how about getting a part time job and writing in the evenings?'

He looked at me as if to say that his closest friend had no confidence in him. Which was possibly true; he had tried and tried for over a decade and was no nearer to breaking through.

More years passed and the situation remained the same. Then one day I got a phone call: 'Robin, I've just made my first film! I sold a script, they'll finish filming it next year.'

'That's great.' I said thinking it was a small independent film.

Guess how much I am getting? he quickly added.

It took me five minutes before finally I hit the number. He had sold his first movie script for $800,000 and the film was a major theatrical release. It taught me a lesson that I've never forgotten about the individual's ability to persist and endure through repeated failure; about the paramount importance of believing in yourself and never quitting; about getting up again, every time you fall. I am delighted and proud to tell you that my friend Peter is today what he always dreamed of being – a highly paid screenwriter.

So let's agree to persist in our journey. Let's agree to persevere along the route towards our own personal successes, large or small, whatever they may be. I hope that I'll be able to help you to create and develop a success habit for yourself. Leave those imagined and self-imposed obstacles behind – right now!

Within you right now is the power to do things you never dreamed possible. This power becomes available to you just as soon as you can change your beliefs.

Maxwell Maltz (1899–1975)

ACHIEVING A BALANCE BETWEEN THE SEVEN PRINCIPLES

You may ask which of the seven essential principles – a clear goal, a definite plan, confidence, no fear of failure, purpose, commitment and celebration – is the most important. In one way, the goal is the most important because without it you are lost. But just as vital, I think, is banishing the fear of failure, because if you can develop the no-fear mentality you will be able to begin your journey; you will not be the one that fear leaves rooted to the spot, whose projects and plans, brilliant though they may be, remain for ever unrealised. Equally without commitment nothing happens, and if you have no sense of purpose the whole experience will be a slog, making success highly unlikely. Finally of course, success without celebration feels like no success at all.

So balance the seven principles carefully. Give priority at the beginning to a clear goal and to banishing fear. In the creation of a plan, although there is often no obvious route, there is always something you can do to begin the process. The important thing to remember is that whatever you do, no matter how simple, it is a beginning. When it comes to the plan, once you've devised it, it will probably take care of itself; and the little steps you take on the path to success will give you all the confidence you need.

Once you have set your goal, ask yourself two questions:

1 Where do I want to go?
2 When do I want to get there?

Perhaps it would be a good idea, fantastic as it sounds, to muffle every telephone, stop every motor and halt activity for an hour some day to give people a chance to ponder for a few minutes on what it is all about, why they are living and what they really want.

James Truslow Adams (1878–1949)

The reason I'm asking these questions is that precisely defining your goal in this way helps you create a clear image of it in your mind. And furthermore once you know the where and the when, *you will* find the how – as in how am I going to get there? – has a wonderful tendency to crystallise before you. Often it just seems to magically appear through apparent coincidences and chance events. In reality you are now fully aware of where you are trying to go, so you will have no difficulty in recognising opportunities when they come your way.

> Once you know where you want to go and when you want to get there, you will discover the how

Think again of those times when you've been racking your brains over a problem, and then suddenly out of the blue, while you're having a coffee or just wandering aimlessly along the corridor looking at fire extinguishers, you have that moment of, 'that's it!'

No man ever became great except through many and great mistakes.

William Gladstone (1809–98)

The solution has suddenly come to you. We read of famous inventors at moments of discovery, or composers scribbling furiously the notes of their new masterpiece. Where does it come from? It comes from within. If we just let our subconscious process get on with the problem, it will probably guide us to the answer all on its own.

When I recommend to clients that they shouldn't worry too much about the 'how' but focus instead clearly on their aim, I'm often met with raised eyebrows – if not downright resistance. Of course, ways and means are important, but I can't stress too strongly that clearly defining your goal *must* come first on the list. Then you can work backwards to your plan.

It is vital in all your endeavours to live in the here and now, to take things one day at a time. You must plan for the future, but be flexible enough to change your plan in the confidence that you will eventually arrive at the destination you have set yourself.

REMEMBER

- There are no short cuts to success – only universal principles to be applied
- All the tools you require to succeed – are within you
- Never give up on yourself – never ever

4

CLEAR GOALS

IF YOU DON'T HAVE A
TARGET IN VIEW, HOW
CAN YOU TAKE AIM?

In the absence of clearly defined goals, we become strangely loyal to performing daily acts of trivia.

Anon.

People who construct their goals in concrete terms are 50 per cent more likely to feel confident that they will attain their goals and 32 per cent more likely to feel in control of their lives.

Howatt, W. A. 1999. 'Journaling to Self-Education: A Tool for Adult Learners.' *International Journal of Reality Therapy*, vol. 18, pp. 32–34.

CLEAR GOALS

The tragedy in life is not in failing to realise one's goals, but in failing to have goals to realise.

Dr Benjamin Elijah Mays (1895–1984)

When young children are asked what they want to be when they grow up, they tell you. They aspire to being a superhero, or maybe they'll settle for astronaut, or a cowboy, maybe even a pirate but in their imagination there's no limit to the possibilities life has to offer.

One never goes as far when one doesn't know where one is going.

Johann Wolfgang von Goethe (1749–1832)

But when they get a bit older, when you ask them what they are going to do when they leave school, they rarely know. Ask and you'll be told, 'I'll find something,' or 'Don't worry about it,' or the ever-popular, 'I'll be OK.' And even when we're long past school age, some of us are still talking in these terms.

Think for a moment about the idea of being 'OK' – do you think it's enough? Do you think it's all you deserve, or do you think you deserve more? If you asked a friend who'd been to the cinema, 'How was the film?' and he replied, 'OK,' would you want to go and see it? Or would you go to a restaurant reviewed as serving food that was 'OK'? I don't think you would. And the reason is that OK *isn't* all right. In all aspects of your life (as in all aspects of your business), you deserve better than OK. What you should be aiming for is great, fantastic, wonderful. But in order to get beyond the OK zone, you need to be very clear about where you want to go.

Remember, the ability to consistently define goals in clear and succinct terms is a common feature of successful individuals. Ask them what they are trying to do and they show clarity and conviction, describing their goals in a way that leaves you in no doubt about where they are going.

When I worked in television, I often had to present an idea for a show to a commissioning editor or a senior producer – this performance is called 'the pitch.' It's when you present your idea for the first time to a potential buyer and you only get one chance to do it. When you pitched a game show, you would describe it in detail, doing your utmost to bring it alive in the buyer's mind; from the host walking on, to the credits and everything in between. Whatever the genre of your programme, you'd describe it in clear visual terms – that's because we tend to think in visual terms, in images. They enable us to describe in great detail what the finished product will actually look like on the screen.

It's the same with both *professional* and *personal* goals. Be under no misapprehension: an objective that is vague and ill-defined will have an indistinct reality in your mind. (So it's no surprise that it won't impress on anyone else either.)

An objective that isn't clearly defined will lack substance

This lack of a firm objective is the number one reason for uncertainty. Uncertainty in turn creates, at a personal level, feelings ranging from complacency and boredom to insecurity and even pervasive anxiety. If you don't know where you're going, it's more than likely that you're going nowhere; and going nowhere is not much to look forward to.

Over twenty years ago, standing on a street in an Edinburgh suburb called Morningside, I was waiting for someone to bring the keys to let me into a house I had rented.

As I stood there, two old ladies walked slowly past. One said to the other, 'It's important to have something to look forward to.' Her friend agreed: 'Oh yes, so important.' Those words have stayed with me, because if we don't have something in the future to aim at we become uncertain, we feel insecure, and the future becomes a frighteningly empty place.

Do be sure that any personal goals you pursue are yours and not ones that someone else has set for you. By contrast, in business, of course, group ownership and collective agreement are essential.

Start by asking yourself, 'What am I doing with my life?' How often have you put this question to yourself? I mean how often have you really sat down and worked at it until you've come up with an honest answer? Very rarely, if at all, probably. People say they are too busy just keeping their heads above water, for many the pace of modern life makes it difficult to aim at anything more ambitious than survival. But ignore those voices, and ask yourself right now, 'What do you want to do with your life, and where you want it to go?' We all want to be accomplished, respected, successful; we want to be admired for our achievements yet we seem to spend so much time running around and *not* doing the most important thing we can do with our time, *thinking* about what it is we want to do. We could make a start simply by converting our worrying time into thinking time.

The good use and the misuse of time and energy are well contrasted in the little story of the two people in the swimming pool, both expending the same amount of energy and splashing lots of water about. But while one is purposefully swimming length after length, the other is in the process of drowning.

Effort is not a measure of progress if it lacks direction

Are you swimming or drowning? It is very important that you use your energy constructively in setting and achieving your goals. It goes without saying that your goals should always be ultimately for good – for the good of yourself, your family, your company, your society, for the world around you. But the most important thing of all if you're going to achieve your goals is – that's right! – to make sure they are clearly defined.

WHERE DO YOU WANT TO GO?

Imagine jumping into a taxi and telling the driver, 'Quick! Somewhere!' (Try it sometime on the way home, and see what happens.) The taxi driver, obviously, would be utterly perplexed. I am amazed how many people, when asked where they want to go, reply: 'I want to make a lot of money', 'I want freedom', 'I want to be successful', 'I want to be happy'. (Do any of these sound familiar?) What's happening here is that they are confusing worthwhile desires and aspirations with defined goals. And though I do know that success is not a fixed destination but rather an experience along the way, it must have a focal point.

But we need to choose that focal point carefully.

I was once told a story about a college football team which, though it had never been particularly successful, became very focused and motivated on reaching the national finals. Throughout the season they played like lions and, against all the odds, they got to the final, only to be very heavily defeated. When asked afterwards why they lost, their coach replied, 'Because we hadn't made winning our goal – unfortunately, we made our goal reaching the final. Next time it'll be to win the championship.'

At a personal level, being very clear about what it is we want to achieve has a major impact on our ability to be successful. When we are young we have many ambitions, but as we get older we tend to lose sight of them, mainly because of difficult life situations. Our young dreams fade; we believe they are now unrealisable. What happens as a result of this is that we never see things through. But there *is* a way of overcoming it. Simply resolve never to stop seeing yourself as achieving those early ambitions.

What you think of yourself is much more important than what others think of you.

Seneca (*c.* 55 BC–39 AD)

To do this, we have to project and visualise a future scenario where we have already realised success. We must be determined not to allow ourselves to get trapped in our current situation just because we like the sense of safety, the feeling of security, it gives us. We must not become rooted to the spot because it's just too difficult, too risky, to do anything else.

So make the effort now and get outside your comfort zone. How far outside is up to you. But like the bird trapped in the cage, you must find the courage, the belief in yourself when the door is opened, to embark on a journey that you will not give up until you've arrived.

Think of our heroes, think of those brave souls who set out, often without maps, to discover uncharted land masses, knowing that there was a new world to be found. You need to experience that same level of belief and excitement at the journey that awaits *you*. Some of *your* route may take you into uncharted territory: see it as the adventure that it is, and embrace it.

HOW BADLY DO YOU WANT SUCCESS?

A young pilgrim was sitting by a riverside with his master. He told the master that for many years he had meditated and sought illumination from God, but he had never come close to enlightenment. 'What must I do to find God?' he asked the master. The master looked at the young man, then pushed his head under the water and held it there for some time. After frantically struggling for several moments against the hands that held him down, the young man mustered all his strength broke free of the master's grip, got his head above the water and started to gasp for breath.

'Why did you do that to me?' he spluttered.

The master replied, 'When your desire for enlightenment is as great as your desire for that breath, then you will be ready.'

The story is told in a spiritual context but its relevance to *your* situation is very clear – you must want to achieve your goal as badly as a drowning man seeks air. You must be absolutely committed, in your heart and mind, to the goal you have set yourself. We're talking about your life here – how seriously do you take it? If you're thinking of just dabbling, of having a go for a bit and seeing what happens – don't bother – because it won't work.

> It's not enough to want. You have to determine

Why do you want to achieve this goal? What are the benefits that it will bring you? You have to understand what those benefits are, because they are your spur to success and will keep you going through the bad times.

Think of all those people that we see running the city marathons like London and New York. Stand at the finish line around the six hour mark if you want to be truly inspired and see the human spirit shine. You will witness the elderly, the overweight, the disabled: people who have determined to complete the 26 miles and 385 yards – however long it takes. Not for them the two and a quarter hours of the gold-medallist – they'll have to keep going for four, five, even seven hours. But they all have one thing in common: they're all going to cross that line. Gold-medallist and septuagerian alike, and everyone else in between– all are determined to make it, determined not to quit. And the reward and the sense of achievement they gain will be satisfaction enough, something they will treasure for the rest of their lives.

I've mentioned before how important it is, when you set out to achieve a purely personal goal, not to share it with anyone who's likely to pour scorn on it. People who regale you with their negative opinions may well devalue your ambition in your own eyes or, at worst, they will simply destroy your dream. Their reasons for doing this are many, but most often they are afraid of being left behind. They may be jealous of your potential success, for that will only highlight their own sense of failure. So do not share your goals with anyone who will do anything other than support you, encourage you, share your dream and look forward with you to its realisation. This same person can be your personal coach, who, when you trip once too often, will help you to pick yourself up and encourage you to never say die.

Set your goal not only in your mind, but also in your heart. Goals that live only in the mind, without emotional commitment, often become little more than wishes that, through distractions or changes in our circumstances, we have allowed to atrophy. For true success, you need to feel a desire to reach your goal so great that it occupies both your head and your heart. When this happens, you will have added purpose with passion to your goal, and there is no feeling better than that.

Goran Kropp of Stockholm conceived an idea, back in 1991, of travelling overland to Nepal under his own steam and then, entirely without back-up, of climbing Mount Everest without oxygen, then returning home the same way. His goal was ambitious certainly; realistic, possibly. Firstly, he did a feasibility study which involved driving the route, then set about raising the £200,000 sponsorship the trip would cost. He started his physical training with the Swedish cross-country skiing team, in order to build up his cardiovascular capacity. On a specially built bike he set out on 16th October 1995, and because it was a totally unsupported expedition he had to carry all his equipment, which weighed a staggering 129 kilos.

After four months and six days he arrived at Kathmandu, from where he set about moving his equipment for the climb towards the base camp; the 73 kilo load could be moved only 50 metres at a time,

with a ten-minute rest in between. For the first time he began to seriously doubt his ability to achieve his objective. The effort needed, he
said, afforded him the single most gruelling physical experience of
his life.

He made the summit on his third attempt, then came back down
the mountain, got on his bike and cycled the 12,000 kilometres back
to Sweden. One year and eight days after leaving he reached home.
Six years later in September 2002, Goran Kropp fell to his death
when only fifteen feet from the summit of a rock climb near Seattle.
His death at thirty-five was a tragedy, but his life was an inspiration,
and our lives are about living our dreams to the full. That is something he certainly did: and as a result he inspired many to reach a
little further and to dream a little bigger.

> Our goals must inspire us, or they will die

We make a living by what we get, we make a life by what we give.

Sir Winston Churchill (1874–1965)

You must want to achieve your goal so badly that neither your purpose nor your passion ever wavers; so that they see you through
those times when your target seems unreachable and you feel like
giving up. Then like the young monk gasping for air you must feel
your goal as a burning desire as important as life itself.

DEFINE EXACTLY

We have discussed the necessity of creating a detailed mental picture
of your goal, but seeing it mentally is not enough. To prevent that
picture becoming fuzzy round the edges, you must also write your

goal down. Writing something down helps the subconscious to form a clearer image of exactly what it is, because the very process of writing encourages a much more forceful definition and generates a more powerful future memory.

However great your ability and concentration, if you have no target to aim at you will be unable to demonstrate it. The physical action of writing and returning daily to the clearly defined goals you have set, reinforces your subconscious vision. The more powerfully you imagine your goal, the more effectively your subconscious will be able to move towards it.

> Imagine getting on a ship and setting sail. As you leave the harbour you ask the captain, 'Where are we going?' He tells you he has no idea, nor for that matter any charts, or navigational equipment. The result is that you might not go anywhere, and even when you do arrive somewhere you won't know where it is, or see it as a place you planned to be.
>
> It's the same in your life, the more you can define your goal, the better.

SEE IT IN YOUR MIND'S EYE

Visualisation is the active engaging of your imagination in order to create a picture of a future desired situation. In other words, it's a scripted daydream. If you have ever daydreamed, you're capable of active visualisation. You may have come across the concept before – perhaps in the context of health care, helping patients to 'see' themselves well again; or in the gym or sports arena, where athletes use it to 'see' themselves winning. I know of salesmen who visualise successful meetings before they enter the conference room – they find this gives them a sense of familiarity when they begin their sales pitch.

Writing your goal down is so effective because it actively programs your brain to an objective; it changes the way you subconsciously perceive. You may have seen the effect that a stage hypnotist can produce by putting people into a trance, and then, at a subconscious level, instructing them to do things. Though visualisation is not a method of self-hypnosis, writing things down helps to ingrain the goal into your subconscious and, once the information is there, the subconscious works continuously to make it a reality.

The brain reinforces its images not just with visual signals, but also with sound, smell and other sensory signals, and the act of writing something down serves as a physical reinforcement. Your wonderful brain, in all its complexity, now sets about achieving the task that you have set it – working non-stop, until it realises its goal, to bring into reality the vision of your future you formed so clearly in your mind.

IDEAS ARE CURRENCY

I do not believe that there is such a thing as a bad idea – an idea is simply an idea. It may be appropriate, it may be inappropriate, but ultimately the task in hand will determine which. Every goal, every dream we have, starts off as a thought, so the more creative our thoughts, the more ambitious our dreams, the more opportunities we are creating for ourselves. When we have a clearly defined goal in our minds that we revisit daily, both by writing it down and by visualising it, our subconscious works non-stop to reinforce that image. Often we are afraid to think big because we fear ridicule, or believe that our goal is too ambitious. Don't be afraid.

Think big, start small

The most remarkable ability we have, the one that sets us apart from other species, is our ability to harness our imagination. It is imagination that has allowed us to overcome huge difficulties, to create great art and entertainment, to discover cures for countless ills, and to dream of things unseen and unmade and make them a reality. If you are asked what your goal is by someone you know you can safely confide it to, make sure you have an answer. In fact, you should have so much to say that your only worry would be boring them with the length of your answer.

> Formulate and indelibly stamp on your mind a mental picture of yourself as succeeding. Hold this picture tenaciously. Never permit it to fade – and your mind will seek to develop the picture.
>
> *Norman Vincent Peale* (1898–1993)

As children we are read stories about wizards and fairies and genies who will grant us three wishes; and as we grow older, we still occasionally wonder what we would wish for if we had those three wishes. I have never encountered anyone who could not tell me what theirs would be, whether practical or fanciful. So apply your mind to it now and set yourself three life wishes. Then stop wishing, and make them your life goals. A wish is simply a dream you hope for but don't believe in; a goal is a tangible reality you do believe in.

Shortly before his death Albert Einstein admitted, 'I know quite certainly that I myself have no special talent. Curiosity, obsession and dogged endurance combined with self-criticism have brought me my ideas.' Whatever level of ambition you have, think of yourself like Einstein as being capable of generating ideas. So encourage, nurture and develop those ideas; they are as worthy as anyone else's. As to whether they are practical you will discover soon enough.

GUARANTEED SUCCESS

As the American evangelist Dr Robert Schuller famously asked, 'What would you attempt if you knew you could not fail? What would you wish for one year from today if success was absolutely guaranteed? And knowing that success was guaranteed, how confident would you feel as you approached your target? With what degree of confidence, and with what kind of attitude, would you tackle setbacks and difficulties? How committed, how determined, how passionate would you be?'

I believe that success *is* guaranteed if we pursue our goals with 100 per cent belief in their achievability; if we understand that success at a personal level is the gradual realisation of our individual goals, then small incremental steps towards our goals are successes too.

> Success is not a destination, but an experience of the journey. Enjoy the trip

Only you can know whether your personal success is a true reflection of the commitment you have invested in achieving it.

This above all: to thine own self be true,
And it must follow, as the night the day,
Thou canst not then be false to any man.

William Shakespeare (1564–1616);
Hamlet, Act III, Scene II

DARE TO DREAM

Nothing was ever created that did not first exist as a dream in someone's imagination. No matter how fantastic, it existed clearly in the mind of the person who imagined it. So what's stopping you from thinking big?

If you look at the largest organisations in the world today, you can trace their origins back to an individual or a small group of people who came together with a common dream. However small they were when they started out, they had great hopes for the future, great plans for the company. And, just as I was advised to when I first went into business many years ago, they were 'thinking big, starting small.'

I am one, but I am only one. I cannot do everything; but I will not let what I cannot do interfere with what I can do.

Edward Everett Hale (1822–1901)

Belief in the dream is everything – otherwise, as we have seen, you predetermine failure. And don't just pay lip-service to that dream: if you don't have absolute faith in it, you'll undermine it completely. It will be like building a house with no foundations. Have you ever heard someone say, 'Well, I hope for the best but I'm prepared for the worst,' or 'Things never work out for me, but I'll give it a go'. What they don't realise when they say this is that they are predetermining their failure – they have created in their own mind the belief that their goal is bound to elude them.

Winners are the people who don't find excuses. They don't procrastinate, they don't go around saying, 'Oh, I can't do that because . . .' They have dropped all their unwanted baggage, negative thinking and self-doubt and are focusing clearly and positively on creating the future.

So what's holding *you* back? Sit down and concentrate on what it is that you would love to happen in your life, no matter how improbable it might appear to other people, and then give it a reality check – is this an achievable goal? Think of it this way: if you aim for the stars and come up short, you still might make it to the moon. Which means at the very least that you will have taken yourself from where you are, towards where you want to be. When you really want to do something you'll find a way – and when you don't you'll find an excuse.

George Foreman, the former heavyweight boxing champion of the world, once said, 'If you don't dream, you might as well be dead.' I think that what he meant was that it is our dreams that give us hope, our dreams that give us, as the old lady in Edinburgh said, 'something to look forward to.' So dream big, start small. And start now.

> People frequently mistake the limits of their own vision for the limits of the world

STARTING OUT

When is the best time to start our journey towards those clearly defined goals? Now! – if not physically, then mentally. Starting any journey or endeavour requires us to act – confidently and promptly – to stop us from hesitating. If we hesitate, we may put things off for weeks, for months, even for ever, and finish up like those old people who, when asked what they would do differently if they had their time again, offer such movingly simple things like: to walk barefoot on the beach, to tell someone they loved them, to change jobs, to set up their own business, to travel more. These things that we may take for granted are chances they didn't take.

Your chance is now. Every day can be a fresh start if you want it to be, so don't look for reasons not to get on with it. Don't say you're going to start your diet, give up smoking, or think about asking your bank manager for a loan in the near future. Do it now.

New Year's resolutions are almost always self-defeating. You may have noticed that if you habitually decide on 1st January that you will stop some bad habit, or start some good endeavour, you generally manage to keep it up until approximately the 3rd or 4th of the month. Inevitably, your brain draws upon the memory of previous failures, so when you determine, as we all have at some time or other, to get up 40 minutes earlier and go for a run, you may stick at it for two or three weeks, but your memory of never succeeding will allow you to justify your failure because, 'that's just the way it's always been.'

Is there a particular aspect of your life that you'd like to be different? Then start immediately, mentally if not physically, to prepare yourself for change. You cannot discover new oceans until you have courage to lose sight of the shore.

Write down all the reasons why you should start now, list all the potential benefits to yourself – this in itself will strengthen your resolve. And as your self-esteem increases from your small successes along the way, so the journey will become more meaningful, the process more exciting, and you will become more enthusiastic, more confident – and happier. The effects are external as well as internal; you'll find that people notice this new confidence, this inner knowledge that comes from clearly knowing where you are going. It's not arrogance, either. You *know* you are going to get there. So begin today. Commit yourself to losing that excess weight, to going for that promotion, to rewriting your CV, to sorting out your relationship.

I want to live my life so that my nights are not full of regrets.

D. H. *Lawrence* (1885–1930)

Live that dream. All it takes is a clearly defined goal that is in keeping with your core values and that you are passionately committed to. As the advert says, 'Do it now!' because you won't want to look back 20 or 30 years from now, wishing you had this chance again.

You have it now – take it!

REMEMBER

- You MUST define exactly what your goal is – in terms which allow you to clearly see it in your mind's eye
- Concentrate on the goal – not the obstacles
- No matter how big or grand your goal – it must be *realistic* and you must *believe* that you can achieve it

5

PLAN PLAN PLAN

IF YOU FAIL TO PLAN
YOU ARE PLANNING TO
FAIL

First comes thought; then organisation of that thought, into ideas and plans; then transformation of those plans into reality.

Napoleon Hill (1883–1970)

Case studies on executives reveal that 98 per cent see their position as the result of plans and strategy and that more than half credit their use of a successful person as an example to help define that plan.

Gordon, Darlene, 1998. 'The Relationship Among Academic Self Concept, Academic Achievement, and Persistence with Self-Attribution'. Phd Dissertation, Purdue University

PLAN PLAN PLAN

Walking home one evening in Amsterdam after a business meeting, a Dutch colleague and I passed a chess café; all the tables had boards on them, and many people were deep in thought pondering their games. My friend asked if I would like a game. Never one to turn down a challenge, I replied, 'Certainly.' When he asked me if I was a good player I told him, jokingly, that I was not just good but excellent (though I think my sarcasm got lost in translation). So we sat down, duly ordered two beers, laid out the chessboard and commenced battle. I played quickly and in a random manner. Martin, on the other hand, pondered long over almost every move, studied the board, looked at me, looked at the board again, then carefully made his reply.

After six or seven minutes he looked me in the eye and said in exasperation, 'You don't have a strategy, do you?' Somewhat sheepishly I admitted as much. 'No wonder I can't work out what you're doing,' he said. 'It's chaotic.' A few moves later, checkmate to him.

In the absence of a plan we have chaos, pure and simple; there's no other way of describing it. Martin had been a chess champion at the age of seventeen: it was inconceivable to him that anyone should play without a strategy, because there are too many variations in chess for victory ever to be left to chance. As we played, he was looking for *my* strategy – hence his perplexity.

In this chapter we will look at the whole issue of strategy: its creation, application and adaptation.

Whenever you buy something, be it a washing-machine, a VCR, or especially a piece of self-assembly furniture, it always comes with instructions. They may, as we often joke, be incomprehensible, but my point is that the manufacturers know that they must supply a plan, a pattern of instruction, to guide us towards the desired outcome.

Planning is as natural to the process of success as its absence is to the process of failure.

Think of a microprocessor used in laptop computers, an extraordinarily complex and sophisticated component. Needless to say, none of its development will have been left to anything resembling my chess-playing style. Every part of its design and construction was planned in detail; the exact specification of each aspect was designed, built, tested and redesigned as often as necessary, until it worked. In a sense, the design and construction of the microprocessor is not so different from making that first bookshelf: first you determine what sort of bookshelf it's going to be, and then you plan a strategy to achieve it. Of course, it's not as complex as making a microprocessor (though at times it may feel like it).

Keep your plan simple, the more complex it is, the more likely it is to go wrong. Think of it like a chain – because a chain is only as strong as its weakest link, so make sure there are no weak points in your plan. And the more clear indicators you include to allow you to measure progress towards your goal, the better – and stronger – your plan will be.

When devising your plan, remember there are two simple questions that you need to answer: where do you want to go, and when do you want to arrive there? Answering these questions about the destination and the time-frame helps you to plan the 'how' process.

There is a giant asleep within every man.
When the giant awakes, miracles happen.

Frederick Faust (1892–1944)

I hope I've already convinced you that when you set out to achieve a goal, it's very important to write down your plan. Creating this blueprint for success becomes a powerfully encoded instruction to yourself. The written plan is a guide to which you should return daily, then examine your progress and, if necessary, adapt your plan accordingly. When you hold a plan only vaguely in your mind, when it's something you occasionally think about but have not articulated well to yourself – or written down, the reference points become unclear and your progress towards your goal is hampered.

Every plan must allow for flexibility. As a chess game progresses, so the players may need to change their strategy. And along with flexibility goes personal commitment: a plan is only as effective as your commitment to following it through, which we will be look at in more detail later.

Let's take an example. Suppose you have identified a very clear goal – to be a travel writer – and believe it to be realistic and achievable. You are prepared to do what it takes and are fully committed to giving it your absolute best.

Where do you start? You start by asking yourself some questions, 'what skills will I have to acquire?' 'Will I need to improve my writing ability?' 'How will I go about getting my work published?' 'Is there anyone who can help me with any of this?'

In finding the answers to these questions you begin to acquire the knowledge you need in order to start creating your plan. You will first have written down your goal – to become a travel writer. Then break that down into a number of smaller goals to be achieved en route. The first goal could be to improve your writing to a level where you are confident enough to begin submitting articles. To do this you may need to join creative writing night classes or a writing group. If you think your style isn't descriptive enough, go and see an English tutor or a published author and ask them if they can help you. In the early planning stages you will often find that much of the information and assistance is freely available. Advice is free. Make sure to identify and write these interim goals down too, so you can return to them every day and check your progress; and if any part of your plan is not working, examine why and change it. Think of it like a road map guiding you to your destination. If the road turns out to be blocked, it can also provide you with an alternative route.

There is only the moment. The now. Only what you are experiencing at this second is real. This does not mean you live for the moment. It means you live in the moment.

Leo Buscaglia (1924–1998)

Constructing a plan is easy. Putting it into practice can be hard because early on there will be setbacks, discouragements and upsets – rejection letters, for instance, or the ridicule of a friend you thought would be supportive. The type and seriousness of the obstacles you encounter will vary in proportion to the ambitiousness of the goal, which is why your complete commitment and self-belief are so important. Occasionally you will come up against an obstacle so great that you genuinely believe you can't overcome it. But there is no obstacle you cannot overcome if you are sufficiently determined.

There is always a way – often it does not appear obvious, but there *is* always a way.

If you really get stuck, look at how other people have dealt with similar setbacks. You'll never be the first person to have encountered a particular problem. Military strategists, corporate strategists, chess players study the strategies of past experts – all of them know that finding out and learning from what others have done in similar situations is a prerequisite of success.

Do the same. Study the strategies used by those who have accomplished what you are seeking to achieve. Learn from their experiences and be inspired by them. Whatever worked for them, whatever made them successful, may well work for you. Make the study of other people's approaches part of your plan.

> If you want to be a great dancer study great dancers, if you want to be a success, study successful people

LEARN FROM YOUR MISTAKES

I said earlier that if your plan is not working, change it. Having a flexible plan means that you are *willing* to change it. The important thing is to be able to learn from your mistakes. All too often people don't; they repeat the same mistakes and end up with the same result.

There was a Russian Intelligence officer during the Cold War, who arrived one day at his friend's house with both ears heavily bandaged. 'What happened?' his friend exclaimed.

The officer replied, 'I was ironing my shirt when suddenly the phone rang, and without thinking I stuck the iron against my ear!'

His friend then asked 'What happened to the other ear?'

'Oh, I did that when I telephoned for the ambulance!' he answered.

Sometimes we get so locked in to one way of doing something – in to one way of thinking, that we believe it impossible to find an alternative.

I also rather like the story of the wise old monk who, every morning before dawn, went to the temple to pray. Each day as he began his prayers, the temple cat would walk in and brush up against him and distract him. Eventually he decided to take some string into the temple and tie the cat to the altar while he said his devotions. This continued every day for many years until the old monk died. Then the young monks continued the tradition of tying the cat to the altar every morning during their devotions. One day the cat died, so they got another one. After another hundred years of cats being tied to the altar, somebody said, 'This is silly – why don't we get a statue?'

So they got a statue and put it at the bottom of the altar, and after another hundred years another monk said, 'This is such a beautiful statue, it's so old, it's such a wonderful tradition – I think we should put it on top of the altar.'

And so as the years went by the monks used to sit and worship this cat, and no one ever really knew why they did it, but it had always been there, so there had to be a reason.

Too often, we just accept the way we do things, without thinking. But don't be afraid to challenge your goals; don't be afraid to challenge your plans; don't be afraid to challenge yourself. If your plan is rigid, if it cannot bend, it will snap. This is why it must be flexible. If the time-frame you originally conceived proves too short, then extend it, reset the date. If, on the other hand, you are ahead of schedule, don't worry about bringing your plan forward – it's your goal, no one else's. If you allow yourself the flexibility to change your blueprint as you go along, you won't be demoralised by changes when they occur. Often the goals we set ourselves are moving targets and so we actually *need* a moving plan – and I don't mean one that makes us weep every time we look at it.

Rules for being human
You will learn lessons.
There are no mistakes – only lessons.
A lesson is repeated until it is learned.

If you don't learn lessons, they get
harder (pain is one way the universe
gets your attention).
You'll know you've learned a lesson
when your actions change.

Anon.

ASK FOR HELP

Casanova lay on his deathbed. Suddenly, there was a knock at the front door and a young Scotsman appeared: 'I must speak to Casanova, for only he has the knowledge to answer my question. It is essential that I speak to him.'

Casanova's doctor replied, 'That's not possible, because he is gravely ill and cannot see anyone apart from his close family.'

On hearing the noise outside Casanova asked that the visitor be let in. So the young man went in and knelt at Casanova's bedside and said, 'Hey Casanova, you've made love to over 1200 of the most beautiful women in Italy.'

Casanova looked at him and said, '1500!'

'All right, all right, 1500 of the most beautiful women in Italy. But how did you do it; I need to know your secret?'

Casanova beckoned him to lean closer, gave him a conspiratorial wink and whispered in his ear, 'I asked them.'

How often in your own life have you failed to ask for something? How often do you complain about things that don't seem fair – promotions that have passed you by, opportunities that have not been freely available to you? Yet in most circumstances all you had to do was to ask.

When creating your plan, ask for information, ask for advice, ask for the help you require. Twenty minutes with an expert or with somebody who has achieved what you are attempting will be invaluable. It could save you months or even years of making the mistakes they made. It is guaranteed to be time well spent. If you were walking along the roadside and a car pulled over and the driver asked you for directions, would you help him? I believe most people would. Isn't it interesting that when strangers come and ask us for help, we listen to their requests and, if we *can* assist them, we will? This is such an invaluable resource: never overlook it. At work, if you want to learn a skill, talk to somebody who has it; benefit from their shared knowledge and experience. And when you've gained the knowledge you want, respect it. It will be an asset that will help to reinforce your vision. Knowledge is power, it's said. But that's not strictly true, knowledge is knowledge. But *applied* knowledge is true power. So act upon the knowledge you glean, just as the people who taught you acted on it.

If you had the chance to go back in your life and ask one person a question, who would it be and what would you ask them? Now determine never to miss such an opportunity again – when you recognise an opportunity, act on it.

When I was being treated for cancer, the professor asked to see me one day when I went for a routine check-up. I figured this was definitely bad news because I had never been asked to see such a senior member of staff before – obviously my sell-by date was up. I went into his examination room, with a heavy heart.

'How are you?' he asked.

Now, I wasn't sure if this was a leading question so I kind of hedged my bets and said, 'Not bad.'

Then he told me why I'd been summoned. With the amount of clinical research he did, he explained, he rarely got a chance to see patients, and he'd asked reception to send him some that day. My name had come out of the lucky dip. Then he asked if I had any questions – and boy oh boy, did I!

Nothing happens until you do something. Asking for help – is doing something

I asked him everything – from things I had read about the latest scientific research, to home-made recipes for curing people of the disease. After we'd talked, he told me to write down any further questions I might have, for next time. So two months later when I went back for my next check-up, I pulled out my thick notepad. And did he earn his money that day! Later I was asked to speak to some young people with Hodgkin's, to share my experience with them from the patient's perspective, to answer their questions about the experience, the treatment and the likely emotional reactions they might expect to have. I became something of a mentor to one of them; somebody they could ask questions of, somebody who would listen, offer encouragement, help set strategies, and keep them focused and positive. This is what I tried to do for them and it's what a mentor should do for you if you can find one – someone you trust and who will share their experiences with you.

I once read that 48 per cent of those who ask for a pay rise actually get one. I mentioned this at a lecture one day and somebody said, 'Yes, but 52 per cent don't!' Talk about negative thinking! I replied that those 52 per cent were no worse off than they had been before they asked, but the point was lost.

Go out on a limb – that's where the fruit is.

Will Rogers (1879–1935)

Asking for help, for guidance, for encouragement, is your responsibility and yours alone. You can't *expect* others to come up and offer you the job or the pay rise you want, unless you first make it known to them that this is what you are after. Your friends, your family, your colleagues, your associates – even strangers – will help you if you ask. They will give you that essential guidance and encouragement that everyone needs on their journey to success.

CONTINGENCY PLANS

It is important, when you plan, to devise a contingency, a back-up plan, an alternative that you can put in place if something fails to go according to expectations. When the SAS put a plan together, it's a collective process; if four men are going on an exercise, then they all share ownership of the planning. And that planning always involves the critical question, 'What if . . .? What if the car breaks down? What if we lose the satellite navigation equipment? What if the helicopter doesn't make the *rendez-vous*? For each and every eventuality they have a contingency plan – which is essential, because it gives them both the practical options that will allow them to complete their objective, and the greater confidence that comes from *knowing* they have those alternative options.

Your goal in life may promise little of the drama of an SAS mission, but I know that it is equally important to you that you succeed. So do make sure you have a back-up plan.

Never mistake a single defeat for final defeat.

F. Scott Fitzgerald (1896–1940)

Ask yourself, 'What's the worst thing that could happen?' Then imagine it happening, and say to yourself, with commitment, passion and self-belief, 'So what? I can overcome that! If necessary, I can start again!' And so you can if you have anticipated the problem and provided yourself with a solution. Then you can deal with it, rather be overwhelmed and defeated.

If you find it impossible to work a way through a particular problem, write it down and share it with a colleague or friend. A fresh mind can often see a solution that you would never have imagined. And there *is* almost always a solution. Sometimes it may require only a small change in attitude. When you're dealing with a situation over which you have no control – such as traffic, weather, or interest rates – a simple change in attitude can help you put it in perspective. Of course, there will always be the rare instance where no contingency plan exists, or where all options have been exhausted, and the only possible outcome is failure. People sometimes say, 'Failure is not an option.' But let's be realistic: failure is always an option. What matters is how we respond to it. That is the measure of our character and of our resolve to succeed in the future.

The gem cannot be polished without friction,
nor the man perfected without trials.

Chinese proverb

Never forget that many of the most successful individuals in history have experienced defeat. They have known failure; they have known rock bottom. And what they've all done is picked themselves up, dusted themselves down and started all over again.

BE CONSISTENT

Your plan is one part of the process of your eventual success. Equally critical is a consistent self-belief and action, a conviction that you are going to succeed. This means that the plan is not just something you say or write down: it is something you live, 24 hours a day.

Act in a manner consistent with success; act as if the success you desire is already a reality; act, speak and think like a winner. Try hard to achieve this consistency: if you do it, it will manifest itself in all aspects of your behaviour and, equally importantly, influence others' perception of you.

> Just sticking to it is responsible for creating more success than you could imagine.

I had been out of work for a while, many years ago, and was suddenly brought up short against the reality of it – I had little money and a mortgage to pay. I called a friend and told him that I was thinking of approaching a major broadcaster but I didn't know the name of the head of entertainment. My friend gave me his name and added, 'He's a lovely fellow, just give him a call and make an appointment – he'll see anyone.'

I rang at once. As it was lunchtime I got straight through, spoke to him and fixed a date. The day before my appointment I called my friend and asked him for some tips to help me impress this fellow at the meeting. He told me to dress casually, act lively and be sure to speak loudly because the man was a bit deaf.

Confidently armed with this information, I turned up next day at his office casually dressed, talking at the top of my voice, and with all the energy of an aerobics instructor in the finals of a world championship. I went into my pitch about who I was and what I had been doing and what I would like to talk to him about, and after a minute and a half of this non-stop onslaught, he put his hand up in a 'be silent' gesture and said, 'Stop! Who are you?'

So breaking off from my planned interview I told him. Then we talked for 40 more minutes in a perfectly normal manner, at the end of which he offered me a job and I stayed there for three years.

The twist is that I found out later that my friend had been joking (some friend!), but I just hadn't realised. The man almost never saw people he didn't know, didn't like people who were too casual or extrovert, and he most certainly wasn't deaf! Yet the curious thing was, I was so convinced that I had inside information on how to impress him that it gave me the self-assurance to act in the manner that is so essential to true success – self-belief – even if my performance that day was a little over the top. On that occasion, my self-belief was consistent with my goal, and as a result my confidence levels were through the roof.

Think of it this way. Imagine walking down the road with your fly buttons open – but you don't know it. You're strolling happily along, talking to your friend, looking into shop windows. And you walk along like this for, let's say, ten minutes. Now imagine somebody pointing out to you that your fly is undone, and then asking you to carry on down the road for another ten minutes. How would you feel? How would you act? Very differently from how you acted when you believed your fly was closed, I think. The point here is that if you truly believe something, the way you talk, the way you behave and the way you think will all be consistent with that belief. So you must believe in your plan and you will behave accordingly. If, on the other hand, your actions are at odds with your plan, don't expect much progress.

I find that the harder I work, the more luck I seem to have.

Thomas Jefferson (1743–1826)

Finally, imagine you have won a wonderful prize, and the award ceremony is going to take place in one month's time. You have been told you are going to get the award, you have read the letter confirming it. You have had your hand shaken and your back slapped – everyone has congratulated you. How are you going to feel and act for the remainder of the month? Will you act reticently or nervously? No! Of course not! You will act in a manner that is consistent with your knowledge.

And so it should be with our own future goals. Believe that they exist in the future, and act accordingly. Your self-belief will manifest itself both in your inner confidence and in your actions.

ENTHUSIASM

True enthusiasm is a marvellous quality. It's infectious; it gives confidence to those around you as well as to yourself. When you are putting your plan together, enter into it with gusto. It will be a powerful reinforcement to your commitment. When you speak to others of your goals, speak with that same enthusiasm, that expression of inner exuberance, an unquenchable positive outlook and an assured belief in your future.

Enthusiasm animates, gives life to our plans. Conceiving and designing our plans without it, is like building a powerful engine and then having no fuel put in it.

I am not suggesting you become extroverted, loud or brash – far from it. But let your enthusiasm – your joyful belief in the absolute achievability of your goal – shine through, because when you do, your success will start to become a reality.

> When a man dies, if he can pass enthusiasm along to his children, he has left them an estate of incalculable value.
>
> *Thomas Edison* (1847–1931)

True enthusiasm is free and abundant. It may be that, when you begin to draw up your personal plan, no matter how simple or how ambitious, the only two things that you can generate for yourself are your enthusiasm and your commitment. But when enthusiasm comes from the heart then true commitment begins and our journey towards our goals start to comes to life, as we take action.

Enthusiasm engages our commitment, and commitment creates personal power

OPINIONS VERSUS FACTS

During a course I was running with a colleague, I started to pick out some faults in a proposal of that I was looking at.

'Robin,' he said, 'opinions are like noses – everybody's got one and I don't need yours.' In fact, his actual words were slightly less polite, but the message was quite clear. All too often, when we are discussing our goals with friends, somebody will make a glib comment based, perhaps, on some personal experience or hidden personal agenda. Unless everyone is vigilant and scrupulous in this respect, it's very easy for an ill-considered comment to transform itself before our eyes into a 'fact', unchecked, unchallenged and possibly quite destructive.

I can recall countless meetings where a loose comment has sent the whole mood – the whole discussion – off at a tangent, causing a poor decision to be reached on the basis of one person's opinion. It is extremely important, when you are creating your plan, to work only with facts. The Natural Born Winner within the child learning to walk works exclusively with facts. Children use tried and tested information to reach their conclusions; they are too young to have been exposed to opinions that can rob them of their goal. This may seem as obvious as the nose on your face, but I am amazed how many plans are nipped in the bud by an ill-conceived comment, by 'an opinion'. Of course, considered, informed opinion can be of great value, but it is still no substitute for fact, for accurate information. All too often we decide not to do something because, at a critical moment, somebody said it wasn't possible – and we chose to believe that person's opinion rather than believe in ourselves.

> Never mistake an opinion for a fact

For example, suppose you decide that you want to start your own business and work for yourself. It's going to involve something you've always been interested in – say, interior design – and you don't know a great deal about it, but your friends say you've got very good taste. They've always been very encouraging of your abilities in this area, and one day you tell them you've decided to set up on your own. Now, I don't know what your friends are like, but I'm pretty sure their reactions will range from 'Fantastic!' to 'You're crazy!' Even your best-intentioned friends may say, 'You've got terrific taste, but you know, you're not really a professional.'

Remember that all professionals were previously unpaid amateurs, who just happened to have the confidence to charge money for their services. So if your friends' reactions are positive, take them on board, if they're negative don't take much notice.

Since it's fact that's important, not opinion, seek professional help. Go and find out what you need to do to become an accredited interior designer. Discover what sort of courses you need to go on, what contacts you need to make, who to speak to. Make all this part of your plan. Go and see people who have succeeded as professionals write down the questions you want to ask them ask to see samples from their portfolios. If you don't have a portfolio of your own, ask them how to go about putting one together. Above all, don't let your good idea stall just because somebody said it's impossible.

Facts, not opinions. I remember an occasion when the difference between the two was really brought home to me. It was when I was a student back in the late '70s, and I was at a rugby club summer barbecue, wearing my best flares. I was returning from the bar at some point when I spilt some beer down a friend's jacket – not a whole pint, but quite enough – and I said to him flippantly, 'Ah, well – that colour doesn't suit you anyway.' (It was lime green, if I remember.)

'I'm going to give you a beer shampoo!' he said as he turned to face me, then proceeded to pour the contents of his glass over my head. When I said that his jacket didn't suit him, I was simply expressing an opinion. When he said he was going to pour the beer over my head, he was expressing a fact.

DO IT NOW

In the last chapter I asked you to choose three things which, if success were guaranteed, you would wish for. I'm sure you had no difficulty in choosing them. The next step, now, is to actually draw up your plan. Sit down, take those three wishes, work out for each of them exactly what it is you want to achieve, then ask yourself when you want it to happen. Put together a time-scale: short-term, medium- or long-term – you decide. Now, what do you have to do to make it happen? What skills do you need to learn? What problems or obstacles are you likely to encounter along the way? What benefits will the achievement of this goal bring to your life? How will you feel when you have achieved it? These are questions you have to identify and ask. Answering them will bring your plan alive.

> The sooner you start, the sooner you finish

You'll think that I've said this often enough already, perhaps, but the fact is that it would be impossible to over-emphasise the importance of writing your plan down. A written plan is such a powerfully remembered tool. Lodged in your subconscious, it will stay with you 24 hours a day, seven days a week, until your goal is achieved. I hardly need tell you by now that this book is all about creating success by design, about creating the life you want, and planning is critical to the success of your goal. So when is the right time to put this plan into practice? Now! (You *knew* I'd say that.) Right now! Not tomorrow – today!

When you get to the end of this chapter, I shall ask you to sit down and write out your goals. Then write down your reasons for *not* attempting them; write down your reasons *for* attempting them; next, concentrate only on the positive reasons and on the benefits of achieving your goals; then, set your targets for each stage along the way.

You will be able to change the dates if you need to, you'll be able to change the plan – that's fine – but what is crucial is that you put it into action *now*! Any delay now will stall your momentum, undermine your ambition, dilute your enthusiasm and commitment.

How many times have you heard people say, 'I'm going to start my own business soon but right now I'm figuring out all the angles, I'm looking into things, I'm checking it out'? All they are doing is stalling – stopping themselves from getting started – because as long as they don't start they can't fail; they are still in their comfort zone. They are afraid

Don't make the same mistake. Stop making excuses, take the plan and start the journey now.

> My own experience has taught me this: if you wait for the perfect moment when all is safe and assured it may never arrive. Mountains will not be climbed, races won or lasting happiness achieved.
>
> *Maurice Chevalier* (1888–1972)

Before moving on to the next chapter, do the following exercise. Identify three goals – one short-term, one medium-term and one long-term. Take your notebook and write them down. Your short-term goal can be something you hope to achieve in one month or less. Your medium-term one can take up to a year to achieve, and your long-term goal can take any amount of time as long as it's more than a year – you decide how long long-term is for you. Underneath your three goals draw two columns. Then write down in Column 1 all the reasons why you should not attempt these goals, all the reasons you *shouldn't* try; and in Column 2 list all the reasons why you *should* try. Now take a red pen, look at both of the columns, and cross out all the negative reasons.

This will leave you with only the positive reasons. Next, determine what you will have to achieve at each stage so that you will be able to measure your successful progress towards your goal. Say your short-term target is simply to be more friendly to people you work with – which might seem a strange ambition, but it would be a big step if it involved changing a pattern of behaviour that you don't much like. Your goal for the first week might be that every day you'll smile at one person, and make a conscious effort to be cheerful when you speak to them, and that when you do so you'll observe their response. In the second week, you'll determine to ask people, 'How are you today?' In the third week, you'll continue to do what you've done in the previous two, but you'll go that bit further by using someone's name when the opportunity arises – perhaps at the check-out counter in the supermarket – so giving yourself a chance to be actively friendlier. And by the end of the fourth week, whatever your short-term goal may be, you'll look back over the last month and feel a tremendous sense of achievement when you realise how far you have come.

How often have you done something new in your life, like learning to ski, swim, drive or speak a foreign language, and thought, 'That wasn't so difficult – I wish I'd done it sooner!'? Well, don't wait until later because now is sooner. Do it now!

REMEMBER

- Create a plan that enables you to see clearly the many short-term goals you need to achieve on your road to success
- If the plan is not working – change it as often as you need to
- A plan without action is just words on a piece of paper – it is no more than a map, but without one you will get lost

6

CONFIDENCE

CONFIDENCE CAN BE
DEVELOPED AND
GROWN, IT GIVES US A
BELIEF IN OURSELVES
AND OUR ABILITIES

Self-confidence is the first requisite
to great undertakings.

Samuel Johnson (1709–1784)

Confidence, in combination with a realistic self-
appraisal, produces a 30 per cent increase in life
satisfaction.

Sedlacek, W., 1999. 'Black Students on White Campuses'. *Journal
of College Student Development*, vol. 40, pp. 538–50

CONFIDENCE

Confidence – or lack of it – is something we can all recognise in others, and if we are honest with ourselves, we know whether we too are truly confident or not. It is an intangible quality, not one you can take a pill for, but it is nonetheless something that you can and must develop. A personal commitment to developing your confidence is a major investment in your future.

> The relationship that you have with yourself is the single most important relationship you will ever have. It is the basis on which you are able to form other relationships

Your self-confidence is a direct indicator of how you feel about yourself.

To say that somebody lacks confidence suggests a flaw in their character, a natural deficiency which inhibits their personality; yet in fact our confidence is something we do have power over. We can develop it, build it up, and use it to help us create our future.

Confidence involves the ability to believe in something without necessarily having any firm evidence for it. The ability to believe in yourself is the foundation of your confidence, and positive experiences serve to reinforce it.

When the English football team had to play against Scotland in Euro '96, the Scots trekked down to Wembley Stadium to play their historic rivals.

They were desperate to win and the English were desperate not to lose. Terry Venables and his English team had been treated so negatively by the media for the preceding two years that their confidence was at an all-time low.

Once the game began, the Scots played as always, with a great deal of passion; and the English defended well. Then the Scots were awarded a penalty, which they missed. Later in the first half, at the other end of the stadium, Paul Gascoigne chipped the ball over the head of a Scottish defender and on the volley kicked it into the back of the net. It was one of the best goals I ever have seen.

What happened next was extraordinary: there was an immediate surge in the team's energy, as though a light had been switched on, with every England player showing a renewed belief in their collective ability. You could see the transformation; it was as if they had grown an extra inch. Their self-belief had been re-awakened; the players felt it and were touched by it, their confidence was back. England took full control, played fantastically and won the game. In the next round they thrashed Holland, and in the quarter-finals they beat Spain on penalties. Then, in the semi-finals of the competition they met the only team in the world with whom they seemed to have a mental block: Germany, the one team in Euro '96 with less imagination but, critically, more self-confidence than any other.

What do the Germans do when they go a goal down in a match? Figuratively speaking, they simply huddle down, look at the situation, and determine to score two goals. In this match however they merely equalised. It was a cruel blow. The game was to be decided on a penalty shoot out. Did England fans really think that a German player was going to stub his foot on the ground? Have his shorts fall down in the run-up? Or balloon the kick over the crossbar? No – such eventualities are almost unimaginable, because from their years of experience the Germans have developed a supreme inner confidence that they manifest externally. Every player in the German team believed that day that they were going to win. In contrast, for years both England and Scotland merely *hoped* they would. Germany, it goes without saying, won the shoot out.

Self-confidence enables us to operate in stressful conditions. Upon meeting a man who had spent seven years in the 1960s as a deep-sea diver in the Royal Navy, I asked him if he had ever been afraid of something going wrong when he was alone 200 feet under water with just a bell-helmet on and an air pipe to link him to the surface.

'No,' he replied. 'I'd done emergency training.'

He spoke these words with such a conviction that made it quite obvious that his training had entirely removed any fears he might have had and given him an absolute confidence in his safety.

One person with a belief is equal to ninety-nine who have only interests.

John Stuart Mill (1806–1873)

We need to create within ourselves the confidence to deal with any mishap that may come along while we are pursuing our dreams of success.

Have you ever noticed a child making a speech? Children are often astonishingly confident; they can stand up in front of a room full of strangers because they haven't yet learned to be afraid. Other people's opinions don't concern them. They've got a good enough opinion of themselves, they haven't developed negative self-beliefs. They are not arrogant either – but be aware that the dividing line between enabling confidence and fatal arrogance is, at times, very fine, and it is important to recognise the difference.

Confidence is based on a belief that finds it roots in honesty, arrogance on the other hand finds its roots in delusion and as a result cannot be sustained or stand close examination.

In this chapter we shall look at ways of developing self-confidence. I believe that *the key here lies in the setting and achieving of simple goals.* This helps strengthen your belief in your ability to achieve; it helps you to bolster your self-image; and it gives you the feeling that you are able to take control.

They say that nothing succeeds like success; and the confidence that success brings is self-perpetuating. I believe you have the ability to develop your confidence to the levels that success demands – and, who knows, maybe win a world championship along the way.

YOU CAN IF YOU THINK YOU CAN

I keep returning to Henry Ford's saying, 'If you think you can or you think you can't, you're usually right.' I love this sentiment because for me it's true. When I look back at my life until I had cancer, the things I achieved were the things I believed I could achieve, while the things I never thought would happen, never did. Why is this? It's because when we create an image in our minds of a future outcome, our subconscious then naturally works towards it; with no conscious awareness on our part, it quietly seeks to fulfil our vision. It was having cancer which created the crisis that made me look at my life. I realised that I had 100 per cent control over my attitude and with that knowledge I had 100 per cent control over how I felt about my life, and I realised that I had the power to change it.

When you believe you can do something, you create a positive image, one of success; when you believed that you can't, you create a negative image, one of defeat.

According to the theory of aero-dynamics, the bumble bee is unable to fly. This is because the size, weight and shape of its body in relation to the total wing spread make flying impossible. But the bumble bee, being ignorant of these profound scientific truths, goes ahead and flies anyway and also manages to make a little honey every day.

Anon.

For evidence, look at the self-belief, the self-confidence, of success-oriented people. One thing they truly believe is that they can achieve extraordinary goals. When Roger Bannister ran the four-minute mile in 1954 he was the first person ever to break what was previously believed to be an impossible barrier; and yet since he made that breakthrough, over 30,000 people have followed in his wake. He didn't just break a record: he broke a limiting belief that many had held to be a fact. Mount Everest, first conquered in 1953 after countless failed attempts, has since been climbed so often that you can now take organised guided tours that, if you are willing to pay the price, will enable you to reach the summit.

But don't feel you have to go and climb Mount Everest: we all have our own Everest to climb. Find out what yours is. Identify it, plan it and climb it.

> Our confidence comes from a belief in ourselves, and can be grown from the achievement of small meanful goals, that grow as we grow

When I was nine we lived in a big rambling house with a three-car garage that was always full of unwanted junk that we had accumulated over the years. One summer's day when I could find nothing to do, my mother suggested I go and tidy it up. I went in and took a look It was so full of stuff that there was barely space for one car. I set about tidying and sweeping, and even began to build a bonfire nearby. After four or five hours I still hadn't made much of an impact, and I was tired. When my father arrived and asked me how I was getting on, I said, 'Not bad.' I'll always remember my mother's response: 'Robin will finish this because whenever he says he'll do something, he always does.'

Now this may have been a clever piece of psychology on my mother's part, but in any event it had a great impact on me. Throughout my life it's been the case, that whatever I've started, I've finished. Be it a journey, a marathon or if necessary cleaning out a garage.

Come to the edge, He said. They said: we are afraid. Come to the edge, He said. They came. He pushed them and they flew.

Guillaume Apollinaire (1880–1918)

I have always had a firm confidence in my ability to endure, and when I commit to things I see them through to completion. The things in my life that I have failed to achieve have been those things that I've believed I would fail at; there have been no surprises.

When we face new challenges or set new goals, we need to believe absolutely that we can meet them, accomplish them. But in all our endeavours, even with the firmest self-belief it's natural for doubts to surface; it's natural to have moments of worry and fear. I was once told by a producer about a famous television star, who used to get terrified before every show. He suffered from the kind of anxiety that is quite natural among performers, but his was particularly acute, and before every recording the producer would have to listen to an endless refrain of, 'Tonight I *know* it's going to go wrong, 'This is the night they'll discover I have absolutely no talent,' and so on. But as soon as the clock neared countdown, the star would rise to the occasion as always and go on and wow the audience.

Self-doubt is natural, even for someone who's had twenty years of success at the top of their profession; but the important thing is to put that self-doubt into perspective. Understand that everyone has these moments, and don't fear them or let them immobilise you. Move through them – they're normal, not major obstacles.

Self-doubt is nature's way of giving us a reality check

See beyond your self-doubt and understand, as you persevere in the pursuit of your goals, that it's a natural stage in the process of change that is part of your journey to success. Is there anyone who hasn't thought, 'What if I make a fool of myself?' 'What if I fail?' Don't let negative thinking undermine your resolve; positive self-belief and a determination to succeed will always overcome it.

When you set out on a personal quest, it's natural enough to ask yourself, 'How can I be sure I'll succeed?' The answer is, you can never be 100 per cent certain that you'll succeed. You might just as well ask yourself, 'How can I be sure I'll fail?'

The truth is that there are no certainties in life. Failure and success are both outcomes that exist as thoughts in your mind. It's the one you choose to believe in that will become your dominant and determining thought, and the one you will move towards.

A man who does not think for himself, does not think at all.

Oscar Wilde (1854–1900)

So many of us, when we face the future, are dominated by memories of our past failures: 'Oh, I'll never manage that,' or 'No point in applying for *that* job – I'll never get it.' But don't allow self-doubt to get a grip on you in this way, or fear to overtake you. Think confidently and believe that you *can* achieve, and then you will automatically behave according to that belief.

HAVE FAITH IN YOURSELF

Faith has been described as a belief that runs ahead of the evidence. Anyone who has been exposed to formal religion will be well aware of the emphasis that is placed on faith, on belief in things unseen. The confidence you need to achieve the future you want depends on the faith you have in yourself. If you create a positive self-belief, with faith, you are maximising your potential to create success.

The man who has confidence in himself gains the confidence of others.

Hasidic Proverb

Those negative beliefs that are holding you back were formed by your past experiences. They are the result of learned behaviour, and you can *un*learn them. But it's no good thinking you can change them at the drop of a hat, that you can randomly construct another set of behaviours without solid foundation. It is crucial to your lasting success, to your happiness and satisfaction, that your belief in your abilities should be consistent with your core values, the personal ethical and moral standards by which you measure yourself. Work against them, and you work against yourself.

The Oracle at Delphi is a shrine 70 miles north-west of Athens where, at the time of Socrates, people went on pilgrimage in order to ask important questions and receive answers from the gods. Above the Oracle is written 'Know thyself.' Without getting too philosophical, it's worth asking yourself these questions: 'Who am I?' 'What do I want out of life?' 'What are my values?' and 'What do I believe I can achieve?'

By answering these questions we give meaning and purpose to our lives, and our journey to the future. The route to success is not a long, straight road with clear signposts at every junction. It can be a smooth three-lane motorway one moment, then a twisting, fog-enveloped mountain path the next. Suddenly lost, you feel at your most vulnerable and uncertain at such times. But this is when your determination and imagination, your confidence in yourself, carries you through. Belief in yourself and in your values will always give you direction and enable you to find a way, even through the darkest moments.

Remember the Child

We are born without prejudice and without any sense of externally imposed limits on our potential. We are born genetically conditioned to succeed in the face of natural adversity, to survive.

We can easily forgive a child who is afraid of the dark; the real tragedy of life is when adults are afraid of the light.

Plato (c. 427–347 BC)

Children are born with such imagination, such inner confidence, that in their minds they are the heroes of a thousand adventures. When that imagination and confidence are encouraged, anything seems possible; but when they are neglected, the child is damaged for life. We have seen the tragic television pictures of the Romanian orphanages where children are left uncared for, without stimulation, without love. If a child's imagination is not developed, if the confidence she should naturally acquire is not fed, she will have no memory of personal accomplishment and hence no positive personal belief. Happily, most of us did experience that sense of accomplishment as children, and the memories remain with us, however deeply buried they may now be – as we grow older, we seem either to forget or to disregard those qualities which once gave us an absolute conviction in our ability to succeed.

Put yourself in touch with the child you were; feel again the sense of wonderment and the belief that anything is possible.

When a child sets herself a goal, she may have no prior knowledge or experience of success; she just believes she can do it – whatever it is. The resources she draws on are her imagination and determination. You have still got that imagination; and though sometimes you may need to dig deep to find the determination, you've still got that too. And just as a child's confidence grows through praise and positive experiences, so does yours. So make it an ongoing process – feel good about yourself and about your personal achievements; and if you do something well, something that pleases you, give yourself a quiet, 'Well done!' (or even a loud one).

PUT SETBACKS INTO PERSPECTIVE

I find it odd when I see somebody with a punctured tyre or who has just spilt a glass of milk getting upset and losing their temper. Life and death are life and death, and we should treat them as such; everything else should be put into perspective. It reminds me of the story of the American tourist on holiday in the north of Scotland, who asked an old fellow sitting on a wall, 'What's the weather going to be like tomorrow?'

Without looking at the sky, the old man replied, 'The kind of weather I like.'

The tourist tried again, 'Is it going to be sunny?'

'I don't know,' was the reply.

'Well, is it going to rain?'

'Wouldn't know about that.'

By now the visitor was pretty perplexed. 'OK,' he said, 'if it's the kind of weather you like, what kind of weather is it going to be?'

The old man looked at the American and answered, 'I learned long ago that I had no control over the weather, so I taught myself to like whatever weather comes along.'

Moral: don't get upset about things you have no control over. You do have the power to determine your emotional response to events. If you *don't* control that, it will control you.

So don't act as if the spilt milk is a life-and-death matter, or get seriously stressed out by a flat tyre; they've happened, they're a setback. But they are small setbacks, and everybody gets them. It's what you do next that's important.

It's not what happens to you that matters; it's what you do about it that counts.

When a setback occurs, don't identify with it. Use it simply as something to learn from

Fail fast and fail often.

Thomas Watson (1874–1956)

In 1985 at seventeen years old, Boris Becker stunned the world by winning at Wimbledon as an unseeded player. He came back a year later and successfully defended his title. The year after that at the age of nineteen on an outside court he lost to an unknown in the second round, and was out. At the press conference afterwards he was asked how he felt. With a wisdom way in advance of his years, Becker replied, 'Look, nobody died – I just lost a tennis match.'

He got it in perspective: it was just a tennis match. Sure, it was Wimbledon; sure, the prize was wonderful; but it wasn't a matter of life or death.

Once when I was very worried about something that was making me unhappy a friend asked me, 'Robin, what were you worrying about a year ago today?'

I looked at him, baffled, and said, 'I've no idea – why?'

'Well,' he said, 'a year from today you won't remember this either.'

Try asking yourself the same question. what exactly *were* you worrying about a year ago today? Can you remember? Probably not.

Concentrate on the here and now, give it your full attention

When something bad happens to you – when a love affair goes wrong or a business plan blows up or the bank suddenly decides to call in a loan – you can, if you choose to, hold on to the experience. You can identify with it, decide to carry it around with you for the rest of your life, like a piece of baggage. But if you do keep those negative memories and their associated feelings and allow them to influence your self-image, all you will do is handicap yourself. You will subconsciously use them as your model for the future – a future that will make you anxious and unhappy whenever we think of it.

The alternative is in your hands: simply learn from the experience, then leave it behind. In other words, drop the baggage.

Remember your reaction to any given event is your choice. So when someone tells me that a certain person makes them angry, I remind them that the certain person does nothing of the sort. They only get angry because they choose to. I point out. Think about it!

No one can make you feel inferior without your consent.

Eleanor Roosevelt (1884–1962)

The grandmother of a friend of mine was, I'm sorry to say, a most lamentable woman. In all the years I knew her, she never smiled; she delighted in other people's misfortune; she was, in fact, a very bitter woman. It turned out that once, as a young girl, she had been getting ready to go to a dance when her father told her to stay at home and look after her younger brother. On that day, she vowed never to enjoy herself again. It was her way of punishing her father, of showing him how miserable he had made her. All those years later,

Learn to forgive – then to forget

the memories of that evening had become her reality: they had become the bag she had carried around with her for her entire life. All she had was her bitterness. I'm trying to show you how very important it is to leave this kind of baggage behind, because if you don't move on, if you don't learn from the lessons that life offers you, life has a knack of delivering other, more painful, lessons, until finally you get the message.

Pay attention to your negative patterns of behaviour – we all have them – negative habits that help to generate failure. Try to identify them and think about how to change them. Finally, prepare for setbacks, so that when they occur you are at least emotionally ready. And when you do hit one, look for the positive. Of course, there are some tragedies from which it is impossible to glean anything positive at all; but one thing my cancer really made me aware of, was how much I loved my family – and I had never taken the time to tell them so. I also decided to stop wasting time and start living my dreams. When I left hospital I set about fulfilling many of them, and to this day continue to do so.

So think of a personal setback that in the end had a happy outcome and draw strength from it when another setback occurs. Remind yourself that when bad things happen, you can deal with them, come through them and see that they rarely are as bad as first seemed.

BECOME YOUR OWN COACH

Do you remember being encouraged by a teacher, a friend or a colleague in something that was important to you? Think back to that moment: how did it feel? I bet it felt pretty good, because at that moment, somebody believed in you. They believed you could achieve, and they let you know it by positively affirming their belief. In the process they helped you build your confidence, your self-image – just as a coach does in sport. Of course, coaches also help examine strategies and focus on finer points of technique, but I believe the great coaches finally motivate by encouragement.

Émile Coué, the French pharmacist and psychotherapist we referred to earlier, was one day asked for a prescription medicine by a very insistent patient who didn't actually have a prescription. Knowing he couldn't dispense the medicine, Coué gave him a sugar pill instead, telling him it was an even better remedy than the one he'd asked for.

Some days later the man returned, full of gratitude, saying he had made a full recovery and felt wonderful. Realising that it could only be the patient's own belief in getting well that had cured him, Coué set about creating a method to help people benefit from the power of positive self-suggestion – and enabled himself, in the process, to do away with sugar pills. In due course, he devised his now well-known formula for those recovering from illness: they should say aloud twenty times a day, 'Every day in every way I'm getting better and better.'

As we know, what the mind believes to be true is held deep in the subconscious. The repetition, of 'Every day in every way I'm getting better and better,' enhanced Coué's patients' recovery. And it worked not only for those who were suffering from psychosomatic problems, but also for others who had clinical illnesses.

Coaches are very good at putting positive affirmations into the minds of the people they work with. So why not become your own coach? Your own encourager? Think of what a coach would say, when you have challenges to face, obstacles to overcome, even just simple tasks to complete. What would your coach say? Well, you haven't got a coach, so make it your job to say these things yourself.

When I was training for a marathon, I entered a three mile race as a build-up. Now, I'll make no bones about it: I'm flat-footed and I couldn't honestly compare my technique with that of a top-grade marathon runner. Anyway, before the end of the second mile I had been lapped. It was a one mile circuit, with guides posted at intervals to make sure the runners stayed on course. Towards the end of the race, when most of the entrants had already passed the finishing line and I was still running with just one or two others behind me, there would be a small burst of applause or a few shouts of encourage-

ment as I passed each guide. And I remember what a huge difference it made. It put a fresh spring in my step and even though I felt
exhausted, their encouragement made me determined not to stop
running until I reached the end.

Be encouraged by your successes. Carry the memories of them close
to your heart, and when a new challenge presents itself, recall them.
And as well as becoming your own encourager, your own coach,
why not do the same for friends and colleagues?

DEVELOPING YOUR RESOURCES

I said earlier that it is worth thinking about who your heroes are
and identifying the qualities you admire most. Having identified
them, you can then consciously seek to develop those qualities in
your own pattern of behaviour. Cary Grant was once asked how it
was that he was always so charming. He replied that, whenever he
met somebody with a quality he found endearing, whether it was
courtesy, humility, a natural kindness or anything else, he simply
adopted it for himself. He emulated the qualities he most admired
in others.

Be on the lookout for people who have achieved what it is you
want to achieve, seek them out and ask their advice. See the help
they can give you as another resource, and aim to develop all your
assets in the pursuit of your personal success.

Do you read much? Statistics suggest that less than ten per cent
of the population read more than two books a year. Now, if you
were to read four books a year, you would have read twice as many
as 90 per cent of the population! If you go to any bookstore you will
find a personal development or self-help section. Taking the time to
read a book that will help you gain an insight into something you
are seeking to do, cannot be time badly spent. If you wanted to
learn to cook Thai food, you would think nothing of buying a book
on Thai cookery; if you wanted to redesign your garden you would
probably buy a book or a videotape that would give you the instruc-

tion and knowledge you needed. So it should be with self-help. Build up a library of books on the subject. Listen to tapes in the car or when you are out walking. Books and tapes will give you knowledge and a foundation, but only the application of that knowledge will give you the experience you need to produce successful results. Continue to ask yourself these two important questions: 'Who do I need to talk to? and What do I need to find out?' In this way you will always develop the resources you need to achieve your goals.

OVERCOME YOUR ANXIETY

We have all felt fear in our lives from time to time, but for many people it's a constant low-level condition, a near-permanent state of non-specific anxiety. Fear in itself is a natural response; it saved our forefathers from being eaten by grizzly bears and sabre-toothed tigers. However, prolonged sensations of fear lead to long-term anxiety, which is a very debilitating condition. It strips you of your self-confidence and your self-esteem, and makes you fearful of the future.

He who fears he will suffer, already suffers from his fear.

Michel de Montaigne (1533–92)

You can be almost paralysed by worry about the future, because you have no concept of what it holds. None of us do. But what you tend to forget is that all these feelings of fear exist solely in your head. Think of it this way. *You* put them there, *you* nurtured them and now you are giving them free range of your mind. But you *can* overcome these fears and you can take steps to do it right now.

Anxiety is not a modern phenomenon. The full version of the *Lord's Prayer* includes the line, 'Protect us from all anxiety.' But if you don't deal with your anxiety and control it, it will ultimately control you, leading to a sense of fearfulness and self-pity. It may even lead to the onset of depression.

For many years I suffered from panic attacks, but I didn't understand why. At the age of twenty-eight I decided that they were going to ruin my life or I was going to have to do something about them. After much searching I found a book called *Self-Help For Your Nerves* by Dr Claire Weekes. The understanding that book gave me – the insight into what I was experiencing, the realisation that there was a very logical explanation for it – had a remarkable effect. It immediately disarmed the emotion that had painfully been holding me back. I mention this here because I know from personal experience that many people do feel a non-specific anxiety for which they can't articulate the cause. What has actually happened is that they have become anxious about becoming anxious, or are anxious about the possibility of having a panic attack. This condition is known as precipitatory anxiety; because your experience of anxiety and panic is that it always recurs, you are anxious about it returning even when you are not actually feeling panicky. And sure enough, in one of life's cruellest self-fulfilling prophecies, it returns.

Anxiety is a thin stream of fear trickling through the mind. If encouraged, it cuts a channel into which all other thoughts are drained.

Arthur Somers Roche (1883–1935)

Leave these negative thoughts behind. Think how much energy you are using up in these feelings of fear and anxiety. Imagine if that energy were being used instead to create positive, life-enhancing affirmations of success.

It is natural and healthy to worry, to have moments of self-doubt. A degree of nervous anticipation heightens awareness when going for a new job, or going on a first date. But if you are convinced in advance that something bad will occur – that you won't get the job, that the date will be a disaster – your nervousness will run away with you and it's odds on that you'll be right. Fear can become a paralysing force in our lives if it strips us of our confidence, of our self-belief. It can develop into a debilitating mental condition.

> Most of our anxiety and fear is about things that *might* happen in the future, things that don't yet exist

If you suffer from any form of anxiety, then believe that you can overcome it and determine to help yourself. Read books, seek guidance, share your problem with friends. If appropriate, get professional help. This will begin your process of understanding and overcoming it; of putting it behind you, once and for all.

When I had Hodgkin's Disease, I drove myself to the Royal Marsden Hospital and checked myself into the ward. I was given a bed by the window in a small four-bed room. The night before the operation, a friend and his father unexpectedly turned up to say hello, then a member of my family dropped in. But by eight o'clock I was on my own. The lights went down and I tried to sleep, but I was somewhat preoccupied. Around midnight ambulance men brought a man in on a stretcher and put him in the bed beside mine. He was breathing through an oxygen mask and complained of being intolerably hot, though it was the middle of December. I offered to swap beds so he could be by the window, telling the nurse that I had no objection to it being opened if that would make him more comfortable. It was not possible, the nurse said, but he thanked me anyway.

It was then that I saw him properly. He was about thirty-five, there were tumours on his face, and he was obviously gravely ill. Next day he told me that he had had cancer for two years, but no treatments had been able to stop it spreading. He had tumours throughout his body and, having had a total blood transfusion, he was now in for a body blast of radiotherapy – a last-ditch attempt, he said.

In due course I was taken in for my operation, then stayed in the high dependency unit for two and a half days. When I came back to the ward his bed was occupied by someone else.

As soon as I was able to get up, I started exploring. I was shuffling along the corridor with numerous tubes in different parts of my body, looking a bit like Frankenstein's monster, when I happened to look into a single bedroom and saw this fellow now sitting in an armchair. He looked great and I popped my head in and told him so. He smiled back and said in the most matter-of-fact manner that the doctors had said there was no more they could do for him. And before I could say anything, he added casually that he was off to the hospice the next day.

In the room were his wife, his children and others who I imagined to be close friends and relatives. Some of them were obviously very distressed. Not knowing what to say, I unbuttoned my pyjama top and showed him my scar, 'Look what they did to me,' I said.

He grimaced a little, 'That looks terrible.' Then there was a rather embarrassed silence on my part because I knew my condition bore no comparison to his plight. Then he looked at me evenly, and said, 'I want you to get well. I want you to beat cancer because it has beaten me. I want you to even the score or go one up. All the best.'

With that I said, 'Don't worry – I will,' and I left the room, upset. I went back to my bed and lay there for a while.

Only later did I realise that I would never again be as fearful about my health and my future as I had been before that day. Of course, I was anxious about certain treatments and their long-term outcome, but what raised my spirits time and time again, when I was down or those around me were suffering, was that we can be such a great support to each other. Though he knew that his life was soon to be over and he would be leaving his family behind, that man thought of me, encouraged me to get well.

Whilst I was updating this book for this new edition, I received a letter, from the Royal Marsden Hospital, telling me that I was being discharged; after eighteen years of going for regular check-ups, after eighteen years of being in remission, I'd beaten cancer. I evened the score. I got one back.

IT'S A MATTER OF ATTITUDE

Since the original version of this book was written, I have come to understand much more clearly the immense influence that attitude has on determining outcome. Indeed it can be demonstrated that approximately 80 per cent of the skills we require to be successful are in fact attitude-based skills. The good news is that we have 100 per cent control over our attitude; in the same way that we can choose our response to any situation, so we can choose to have a positive or a negative attitude to life.

When you examine the seven principles of Natural Born Winners, it holds true that 80 per cent are attitude-based. Planning is perhaps less so – it requires some clarity of thought and time management, both of which are skills that can be acquired. But the rest – goal-setting, confidence, purpose, no fear of failure, commitment and celebration – are very clearly to do with attitude.

The last of human freedoms – the ability to chose one's attitude in a given set of circumstances.

Viktor E. Frankl (1905–1997)

The pursuit of success will be deeply affected by your attitudes and expectations, so the simplest yet most immediately effective way to turn this to your advantage is by recognising and accepting full responsibility for them. Don't blame others for the way you think. It is your mind; make it work for you.

Choose to have a positive attitude, see the positive in every situation, be positive around others and you will find that your behaviour follows. And perhaps more than your behaviour – perhaps the world will change too. One study on the notion of luck, found that people who perceived themselves to be 'lucky' had, in general, positive attitudes to life, while those who considered themselves 'unlucky' had the opposite.

That comes as no surprise to me.

Do you know anyone with a negative attitude? Permanently pessimistic, always seeking to burst your dream. Nothing is ever right for them, they suspect the world is especially cruel to them; if they won the lottery they would complain about having to bank the cheque. Do you like hanging around with them? Do they cheer you up? Do they make you feel good? And finally do you want to be like them? Please say no.

You control your attitude: determine and understand that it will keep the sun shining in your soul, it will give you a winning outlook and it will make you a better person. And then you will discover that happiness is not found in things outside us, it is within us, for the person we chosse to be, we become.

Human beings, by changing the inner attitudes of their minds, can change the outer aspects of their lives.

William James (1842–1910)

BE ALL THAT YOU CAN BE

Whatever task we may be facing, it's natural to have negative thoughts about the challenge ahead Maybe it's something as simple as being about to play a game of tennis and thinking, 'Yeah, it will probably rain,' or 'I'm bound to lose.' Do not give value to those negative thoughts: they do not define you, they are not a part of

> You are fully responsible and control your attitude completely. Make it your number one resource

you; they are simply thoughts that you allow to exist in your mind. If you do give value to them, they will begin to dominate your outlook. So if you are going to create a dominant thought, make it a positive one.

An advert for one of the military services in America used to have as its slogan, 'Be all that you can be.' I like that notion very much: you owe it to yourself to be all that you can be, to realise your fullest potential. And you can start the process now by abolishing your negative thoughts, by simply not dwelling on them. When you have a negative thought, focus immediately on a positive one. They say that if you want others to love you it is important to love yourself. It's equally true that if you want others to believe in you, you must first believe in yourself.

But you will not begin to believe in yourself, or develop your confidence, by associating with the negative, by thinking yourself to be less worthy or less capable than you truly are. To that end, avoid negative people – people who, whenever you tell them you are going to do something, immediately pour scorn on it or pull a long face. Avoid them.

Visualise strongly the success you desire and when negative thoughts arise simply ignore them. Remember: the you you see is the you you'll be. How you see yourself, how you visualise yourself, is also what you will be seen as and ultimately become. Fall hostage to negative thoughts and a poor self-image, and you will fail. Abolish those thoughts, build strong self-belief and focus on the positive, and you take a huge step towards success.

In the 2003 Rugby World Cup, Australia tied the match in the last kick of normal time. The Australian fans were ecstatic. England had entered as the favourites and here they were being beaten by the home nation. What happened next?

England stuck with its plan, the players kept a powerful belief in their ability to win, they didn't panic, they didn't consider losing. I read many interviews with those players. They all talked about believing that they were going to win. They focused on the outcome they wanted, they concentrated on the positives and when the opportunity to win came, they took it.

They focused clearly on what they were going to do and they did it. They might well not have done it – but because they believed they could and because they visualised clearly the outcome they wanted to achieve, they greatly increased their chances of creating that result. You can do the same thing, and in the process build up the confidence you need to see you through future challenges.

REMEMBER

- Confidence grows within us as we realise goals – set and achieve small goals
- See yourself as a positive and good person – then become that person
- Learn from your mistakes – they are lessons you learn from, not experiences to identify with

7

PURPOSE

IN PURPOSE LIES THE
REASON WHY – IT
GIVES MEANING OUR
OUR GOALS, AND FUELS
OUR PASSION

Great minds have purposes, others
have wishes. Little minds are tamed
and subdued by misfortune; but
great minds rise above them.

Washington Irving (1783–1859)

When end-of-career managers discussed their
relative success and moments of peak performance
during their careers, more than half spoke in terms of
the significance of personal fulfilment.

F. Thornton, G. Privette and C. Bundrick, 1999. 'Peak
Performance of Business Leaders: An Experience Parallel to
Self-Actualisation Theory'. *Journal of Business and Psychology*,
vol. 14, pp. 253–64

PURPOSE

I have often read and heard it said that man's greatest search through life is a search for meaning. Throughout history, philosophers have sought the answer to the fundamental questions: why are we here? What is it all about? What order or purpose can be found in an apparently chaotic and random world? On the other hand, there are those who have already found their answer – who have found their clear sense of purpose and come to a deeper realisation of meaning in their lives. These people are not the sum total of what they wear, what car they drive, or indeed how much money they have. Their deeper sense of purpose does not come from external factors , it comes from within.

> Look for a benefit that goes beyond material rewards

Irrespective of what you believe spiritually – whether you are a devoted believer in God or a committed atheist – we all have to accept that there are natural laws which govern the universe. For example there is the law of gravity, which can be demonstrated very simply in the laboratory. There are the natural laws behind electricity, which don't change. The fact that we cannot see them does not mean that they doesn't exist; no one has ever seen electricity, no one has ever, indeed, seen gravity, yet we have all witnessed their effects. Similarly no one has ever seen love or hate, and yet we are all aware of their consequences. What we have seen are the effects of love and the effects of hate. Now I believe the same is true of success – that it has its own natural laws, whose effects we see when we achieve success. When we align our purpose to the natural laws of success we can use them to enable us to manifest our goals. Does this sound a wee bit too esoteric/new age or just plain weird? Well I had better put my hand up quickly here and say that many years ago, I was a thoroughly cynical person – not your run-of-the-mill casual doubter, but a world class 'know-all' who was suspicious of anything unscientific or vague. I would have scoffed at the notion that there are natural laws and that to create personal success we must use them or just let them work for us. So I completely understand that you might think this is science fiction or just new age nonsense. I know I did. Big time.

> ## All truths are easy to understand once they are discovered; the point is to discover them.
>
> *Galileo* (1564–1642)

Let me put it to you in another form: does something not exist simply because you don't believe in it? If you jump off a tall building because you don't believe in gravity then it is likely that you'll find at your demise that your disbelief was not sufficient to save you. You may choose not to believe in electricity. So in a thunderstorm you would happily walk around with a very large umbrella, above your head in the middle of a wet field, until you are struck by lightning. Or you could jump off the building with a healthy respect and understanding of gravity and use a parachute to return you to earth safely.

> Because you don't believe in something doesn't stop it being true

I did admit just now that for many years I was a very cynical fellow who dismissed the idea of any natural law relating to success as rubbish masquerading as wisdom. I must now confess that I have myself had enough subsequent experiences to realise that I was just so very wrong. This isn't my evangelising or trying to sell you a bogus theory. It's simply that I've become fully aware that some things just *are*. Whatever goals you have, they will be realised much more quickly and effectively if they have some deeper meaning for you. The purpose doesn't have to be unique or overwhelmingly ambitious, it doesn't have to be ridding the world of disease or saving the whale. But it must have meaning to you. Why? Because purpose is the thing that will keep on burning, that will help us maintain commitment, that will make us feel good at what we are doing and what we are trying to achieve. It will enable us to go the extra mile. It will give our actions a necessary sense of meaning. It will give us inner satisfaction. It connects us to the natural laws of success.

Truth exists, only falsehood has to be invented.

Georges Braque (1882–1963)

Have you ever been involved in an activity or endeavour where you couldn't help thinking, what's the point? As a student, did you ever find yourself stacking supermarket shelves at three in the morning, when they were effectively already full? Have you ever found yourself moving a pile of rubbish, or going through a huge index of filing cards when you knew there was no real point?

> When I was at university I had a job one summer with British Rail, based in Glasgow. I worked in the paint squad. Our job was at night, once the electric power was switched off in the overhead cables, to climb 30 foot ladders, without any safety harnesses, I hasten to add as there were no properly enforced health and safety regulations – don thick rubber gloves, and then paint the metalwork with a protective coat of aluminium paint. It was mind numbingly tedious and potentially dangerous. One night a diesel train came through on a section of track we'd been told was closed, while I dangled on a wire just fifteen feet above. I still feel dizzy at the thought.

Most of the guys I worked alongside were unskilled, many with colourful pasts. They had had very underprivileged lives; hardships and injustice were common themes. There was one fellow called Matt however, who was different.

Whilst the others complained, he said nothing much but had a great deal of presence. I now recognise that was the inner confidence that comes from a strong feeling of self-worth. He was immensely self-assured. One night on our way to the track, someone threw a pair of rubber gloves out of the back of the truck. We arrived, unloaded, collected our ladders, paint and brushes, put on our boiler suits. Matt looked for his gloves and asked if anyone had seen them. A collective 'no' and shaking of heads followed, certain people avoided eye contact. Matt didn't complain, he picked up his ladder, paint and brush and went off to his allocated part of a bridge or electric support that system, that we were to paint through the night.

The next morning we gathered at base before the power was switched back on and all started throwing our equipment in the back of the truck when Matt appeared, smiling – that knowing smile of simple self-assurance. He held up his hands like a magician who's finished a conjuring trick, or a waiter awaiting inspection from the maître d', he displayed them almost theatrically and he said, 'Look lads, not a drop,' and indeed there was not a drop of paint on his hands. His section had been beautifully painted and the rest of us just looked like we'd fallen into the pot.

I asked him later how he had managed to work all night and remain paint free. 'I am a time-served painter and decorator,' he answered and then he added with a knowing wink, 'A real painter.' I understand now, that for him, painting might just have been a job – as indeed it was for us, but he took pride in it and perhaps on that night he demonstrated, if only to himself, that he still had the ability to do the job to a level of excellence and perfection that was faraway beyond our abilities or our imaginations.

BE SIGNIFICANT

At a superficial level, most people will go through life without thinking too much about it, then one day, before long, it's too late. I'd like you one day soon to sit down and imagine your funeral: write the eulogy that you would want to be said at your funeral, think of what achievements you'd want to have mentioned; the person you were; the joy you brought and the success you enjoyed.

My father was a family doctor in Glasgow and he died when he was only fifty-two years old. It was a combination, I believe, of hard work and stress. He was a single-handed general practitioner. He had 2,100 patients and when he took time off, he had to pay another physician a fee to cover his practice and look after his patients. When he died he had a small overdraft in the bank that had been his permanent companion for many years. He'd worked hard to give his children a good education and though we never had many holidays, we'd had very happy childhoods. And yet when he died I was unhappy because I felt that he'd been short-changed, that he hadn't been truly successful. He'd worked hard in a suburb of Glasgow, serving the needs of his patients, but had nothing really to show for it. For all the years I saw him looking through new car brochures he never owned a new car; he bought one suit a year to replace the well-worn one that he had purchased the year before, and the same went for a pair of shoes.

Many people went to his funeral, in fact the church was full. Amongst the congregation were patients, none of whom I knew, and I doubt any of my family did either. After the service a number of them came by and paid their respects to my mother. I didn't pay too much attention to it at the time, but much later, when I was speaking to my mother about the funeral, I asked her about the patients and what they'd said.

Apparently one woman had told her her daughter used to have bad eczema on her hands, she was so embarrassed by it she was unable to work. My father prescribed medication and suggested she wear linen gloves, both to speed up the healing process and stop her feeling self-conscious, but the girl's family were too poor to afford the gloves. Even though he had little money himself my father took out his wallet and gave the mother enough to buy a couple of pairs of gloves, insisting it was a gift and there was no need to repay him.

Other people recalled how he would regularly visit those who were dying or for whom little could be done, simply to comfort them and their families. I remember as a boy, sitting with him outside a pub one summer evening when he struck up a conversation with a middle-aged couple. When they learned he was a doctor, the fellow asked him to look a skin rash on his arm. My father had a look, then gave me the keys to the car and asked me to get his medical bag. He wrote the fellow a prescription and re-assured him that he would be fine. These are not just the emotional memories from my childhood tinged with a saintly character – he was very human and could be as stubborn as he was compassionate. But the point is that he really cared about how people felt. He took great care of others (though not of himself ironically), for no other reason than because it was something he loved doing. He was doing what came naturally: he was living his purpose.

To forget one's purpose is the commonest form of stupidity.

Friedrich Nietzsche (1844–1900)

What I came to understand is that my father, though he never owned a brand new car, was in fact a very wealthy man – he'd created significance. I've learned in life that you cannot help another person without truly helping yourself. My father's purpose, behind the hard work that he did, was to make a difference in the lives of others – a positive difference to their health and their quality of life. No doubt many will think that a doctor is an easy example – they do wonderful work, they heal the sick, they obviously improve people's lives. I just stack shelves in a supermarket, I just run a bicycle repair shop, I just work for a small IT support company, you can't compare that with what doctors do. Don't believe it. I know doctors who don't enjoy medicine, who find patients tiresome and would rather be doing something they loved, something that gave them a sense of purpose, if only they could discover what *it* was. I know however that what my father did every day of his life was to live in accordance with his purpose and do his best by it. He did the very best he could for the people he was in contact with – it merely happened to be in the arena of health. I believe we all have the same capacity to make a difference as we engage everyday with people with whom we come into contact, personally and professionally.

All actions have consequences. Some we never see or get to know about. Seek always to create benefit to yourself and others

We talk about people who lead meaningless lives and the tragedy of those who commit suicide is often accompanied by profound feelings of meaninglessness. Yet there are others who, no matter how humble their work, don't identify with the job itself: their sense of meaning and purpose comes from helping others. Let's return to your goal for a moment. Ask yourself honestly, does it give you a strong sense of purpose? What lies behind your goal?

The man without a purpose is like a ship without a rudder – waif, a nothing, a no man. Have a purpose in life, and, having it, throw such strength of mind and muscle into your work as God has given you.

Thomas Carlyle (1795–1881)

PASSION

Many years ago I gave my first public seminar. It was about an area in which I always wanted to develop my career – peak performance, motivation and developing human potential. I wrote and researched my material, and then I advertised the course and hired a room in a hotel for two nights. I can remember it as clearly now as if it were yesterday. In the audience for my first seminar there were exactly six people. Three girls had called through a temporary employment agency. They wanted to attend but they had no money and their bosses wouldn't pay for them. Don't worry, I said, in an act of self-less generosity, you can come for free! And then a journalist rang and said she wanted to come and do a review of the course. A friend of mine got in touch and I invited him to sit in to make up numbers. And then another friend also agreed to come and help swell the crowd.

Great ambition is the *passion* of a great character. Those endowed with it may perform very good or very bad acts.
All depends on the principles which direct them.

Napoleon Bonaparte (1769–1821)

So there I was my first seminar, with no paying customers and los-ing money on the event. I had a bill for £200 for the room hire, and even worse there was a journalist to review a talk I had never given before. My nerve nearly gave way, I was demoralised by the debt and I didn't know what to do, but it never crossed my mind to can-cel. That was never an option. I recognised that to achieve the goals and dreams I had set for myself, I had to stick to my purpose, pas-sionately believing that the experience would serve me well in the future. My goal was to be a person who impacted positively on the personal development of other people. That was my deep, heartfelt purpose then, as it is today. I could run away from the failure, the humiliation and the debt, I could run away from the fear of failure and ridicule, of a bad review in the press, but try as I might, I couldn't run away from my deep sense of purpose. The event was a success, the journalist gave it an excellent review, and the next event two months later had seventeen paying customers. When you have passion for your purpose, you can create magic.

Find your purpose and pursue it with an unquenchable passion

I believe our purpose is ultimately spiritual – that it is about learning to love and be loved unconditionally. Our passion is what converts purpose into action. A strong sense of passion will underpin our purpose, a strong sense of passion will underpin the goals we seek to realise. Our sense of meaning will be manifest in our service to others, to our community, our colleagues, our customers, our friends and even strangers. It will enable us to achieve our goal whether it's financial freedom, personal security, or even love. But whatever it may be, finding your personal sense of meaning is the route towards it.

Other thoughts on finding Meaning

Meaning, I believe, is to be found in moments, not in things. When you remember happy times, it will be due to a powerful emotional connection to an event. At the end of our lives I am sure that we look back and review and reflect upon the time we had on this planet. We won't remember the cars we drove, the shoes we owned, the jewellery we had, the houses we lived in. We will remember the moments we created, experienced and shared in. We will remember our first day at school, our first kiss, the day we got our first job or our first pay cheque, the day we fell in love, the day we said 'I do'. We will remember the birth of our children or the death of a loved one. We will remember the times when someone put an arm around us and said, 'Well done, that was fantastic,' and the time we were deeply painfully let down by someone we cared about. These are moments that have real meaning in our lives. So create moments for yourself and others, give meaning to the activities you pursue and in so doing you will create and express your strong sense of purpose.

I don't want to be overly prescriptive about what is meant by purpose: it will be different for different people. For some it involves material things, for others spiritual, or a combination of both. It may take the form of praise, glory, appreciation, validation, security, living life to the full, but it need not be exclusively meaningful and altruistic. Some people find purpose in personal vanity, fame, power, invincibility and other ego-related states.

Wherever we find it, purpose is the deeper meaning behind our motivation, because without purpose our motivation is at best a chore, a hardship, a measurable amount of work that we have do and we don't enjoy. When you find the purpose behind your goals, you will have found your motivation. When you're motivated by something greater than basic egotistical or material need, the effort you'll be willing to put in will be infinitely greater than if there'd been no purpose.

If you ask a high achiever or a person of great inner confidence why they do what they do, I'm pretty sure you'll find they say it's because they have a passionate desire to succeed. They have a sense of personal fulfilment and they have found meaning or purpose in the actions or goals they are seeking to achieve.

It is sad to realise that around 65 per cent of people who work don't know why they work. Obviously they work to earn money and they know they need to have a job to earn money, but nothing deeper than that. I doubt very much if they will feel true success. However I guarantee you, if you take the time and honestly scratch deeply enough, you will find your purpose in life.

My purpose is to make a positive difference to as many people as

I can in my life. Not just the audiences to whom I speak or the people who read my books, but to strangers met on planes, harassed serving staff in restaurants and under-appreciated shop assistants; or sharing a moment with a taxi driver, returning the smile of a child just holding a door open for someone. Saying to a stranger with a big smile on my face, 'Good to meet you', or, 'How's your day been?' – and really mean it.

We have seen that for the individual to achieve success in life, we must be clearly focused upon an outcome. The deeper reason and meaning behind that outcome is where we discover the motivation and purpose. It becomes a fuel that will see us through the hard times. Have you ever seen a crime movie, or a tense police drama? At some point a suspect is taken in for interrogation. The basic process is borrowed from the real police and the interview normally begins with, 'Why did you do it?' A great question, as it enables the police to identify motive. So if we can find out why we do things, then we'll have a much better insight into our personal sense of purpose and motivation.

A champion needs a motivation above and beyond winning.

Pat Riley (b. 1945)

For many people and organisations money is the primary concern, and the primary motivator – or at least that is what we are led to believe. However, research reveals that the primary motivations for individuals list both appreciation and a sense of involvement ahead of wealth. When I ask audiences 'Why do you work?' Someone always shouts out, 'Money'. So I ask 'How much?' How much money is enough? Five million, ten million, 500 million? Most people say they want to make enough money to live comfortably for the rest of their lives, but £500 million on a desert island wouldn't be as useful as basic survival and boat building skills. Purpose must find its voice at a deeper level of resonance in our lives. So money, I believe, is not our purpose, it simply provides us with the opportunities to reach our goals.

> Crises forces us to change – the direction we choose to go in, is up to us

Creating Wow

Have you ever experienced great service? I don't mean warm, friendly, 'Hi how are you?' – I mean 110 per cent of excellence, a moment of Wow! I have, but only on a small number of occasions, and they haven't necessarily been at five star hotels, top class restaurants or in the first-class section of an airline. I've experienced it from a shop assistant in a small town in Scotland, I've experienced it in a small family-run hotel in Italy. How does it manifest itself? It is as though the person serving me takes it upon themselves to be personally responsible for the experience I have with that organisation. When we say nothing is too much trouble, it is not a cliché; it is something businesses understand and act on. It is doing with empathy and care whatever it takes to create for another the greatest possible experience – to make it wonderful.

> People forget what you say and do. They never forget how you made them feel

We should create wow for ourselves, and make ourselves feel good about who we are, what we do and how we do it. Not simply something we do for other people, we should do it for ourselves too.

No regrets

Over the years I have met people in the later stages of their lives who lament that they never really, truly found their purpose. If they had success it was due to being in the right place at the right time. They might have achieved lofty heights in the corporate world, but – they never really had a clear sense of purpose – it was just a job that they did well, and in many cases enjoyed doing. Then they say that what they really wanted to be was a journalist or a farmer, a teacher or a musician. There is nothing I can say to these people as their sense of purpose is their responsibility. To have missed it is a personal misfortune. They have missed the fuller life that they might otherwise have had.

> Regret for the things we did can be tempered by time; it is regret for the things we did not do that is inconsolable.
>
> *Sydney J. Harris* (1917–1986)

Please do not think that I'm being judgmental. I only know this to be true: when you find the meaning that drives you towards your goals, you will unlock a force that nothing can hold back. For some people – parents for instance – the purpose and passion is very obvious: to care for their children.

For many others it is not obvious at all, yet if we look at the things in life that are important to us, we should pursue them with the same sense of purpose and passion a parent feels for their child.

We have one life, so make sure you live it fully.

REMEMBER

- Behind every goal there is a purpose – discover yours
- Purpose will give you the drive to continue through setbacks and disappointments – it comes from within
- Be passionate about your purpose – you will create significance in your life and make a difference to the world

8

No Fear of Failure

SUCCESS WILL TEACH
YOU NOTHING, FAILURE
IS YOUR TEACHER.
LEARN THE LESSONS

Courage is resistance to fear, mastery of fear – not absence of fear.

Mark Twain (1835–1910)

Researchers have found that a fascinating change takes place in schoolchildren. When they begin their studies, strong and weak pupils show an equal willingness to ask questions when they do not understand. However as they get older and begin to understand their relative position in the class, students, especially weaker students, become reluctant to ask questions and reveal what they do not know.

Butler, R. 1999. 'Information Seeking and Achievement Motivation in Middle Childhood and Adolescence: The Role of Conceptions of Ability'. *Journal of Developmental Psychology*, vol. 35, pp. 146–63

No Fear of Failure

The fifth principle of success is no fear of failure. This is not to suggest that we should bumble along with an attitude so positive that we are blind to the problems and obstacles that are bound to come our way. Nor of course do successful people want to fail – quite the contrary! – but they accept it is as reality and do not allow fear of failure to get in the way of trying. But it is important to recognise the difference between those problems and setbacks that are real and can harm us, and those that we imagine, those that exist solely in our minds.

When we set out to achieve any goal we should begin by visualising a positive outcome. But as we move towards our objective and encounter difficulties en route, it's easy to grow fearful that our desired outcome will not materialise and that as a result, we will suffer some harm, be it financial or personal. Often in our lives we are in such a rush to get to somewhere that we lose sight of exactly where we want to go, and it's then that we start using loose, vague terms to describe what it is we are trying to achieve. We talk of acquiring security, financial freedom or happiness, or of developing the business. But unless we keep hold of that original clear vision of exactly what it is we want to do, we can easily get lost in the day-to-day problems. They become even larger in our minds, ultimately turning into barriers to our success. As Franklin D. Roosevelt said in 1937, 'We have nothing to fear but fear itself.'

Many high achievers and self-made millionaires are, by nature, problem-solvers. They look for solutions, not more problems. Their style is based upon enthusiastically sharing the vision of what they are trying to achieve and looking to other people as well as themselves, to find the solutions. If you truly believe that you are ultimately going to succeed and are committed to the process, then you too can choose not to identify with problems along the way, but to take the view that you will overcome any obstacle. This is the positive attitude to failure: acknowledging it, learning from it and trying again.

What is the difference between a positive and a negative attitude? One, determined to succeed, shrugs off failure and gets on with the job in hand. The other is fundamentally alien to success, and in consequence accepts defeat.

> The truth that many people never understand until it is too late, is that the more you try to avoid suffering the more you suffer, because smaller and more insignificant things begin to torture you in proportion to your fear of being hurt.
>
> *Thomas Merton* (1915–1968)

It's so important that you care, and it's also important that you have faith in your ability to recover from setbacks. Failure is never final unless you determine it to be so. Walt Disney was bankrupt and recovering from a nervous breakdown when he made *Steamboat Willie Goes to Hollywood*, the cartoon featuring for the first time the character now known as Mickey Mouse. Disney later said that his bankruptcy had afforded him his greatest lesson in life. Financially speaking, when you hit rock bottom there is only one direction you can go – up.

When you understand that often the single biggest barrier you face is self-imposed, that it exists only in your mind, you will find a fresh perspective that sees opportunities more clearly. I don't propose that you neglect your responsibilities or ignore real threats; but I do ask you to differentiate clearly between the real and the imagined.

Be aware of the real. Ignore the imagined

I believe that, when we look at the seven principles of success, it is fear of failure that stands out as the one with which most people have difficulty. Fear has the ability to paralyse us into inaction, and all the planning in the world will be unable to overcome that. Our confidence will be stripped, our purpose and commitment unrealised, and our goal will fade away over the horizon. So it's imperative that we learn to have no fear of failure.

It is not the critic who counts; nor the man who points out how the strong stumbled, or where the doer of the deed could have done better. The credit belongs to the man who is actually in the arena; whose face is marred by dust and sweat and blood; who strives valiantly; who errs and comes up short again and again. Who knows the great enthusiasms, the great devotions, and spends himself in a worthy cause; who at the best knows in the end the triumphs of high achievement; and who at the worst, if he fails, at least he fails while daring greatly;

so that his place shall never be with those cold and timid souls who know neither victory nor defeat.

Theodore Roosevelt (1858–1919)

DON'T QUIT

We have learned about the effect of attitude and that the 'don't quit' attitude of the winner contributes significantly to his success. Sometimes, when we begin the long journey towards personal success, our determination is our only resource; it may be what keeps us going, our only hope. Look back at your life so far and identify something you very much wanted to achieve, and that through your own efforts and without any assistance you did achieve. That's clearly something to be proud of. All too often, though, when we look to the future we recall only our failures. So look back and clearly identify all the successes you can think of, however small. And use those memories to boost your belief in your potential to succeed again.

Those who try to do something and fail are infinitely better than those who try to do nothing and succeed.

Anon.

It is all too easy to quit. It's the easiest thing you'll ever do, it just requires that you say two words 'I quit'. It puts off the problems and the suffering until another time. The excuses we come up with seem fully justifiable; and our colleagues and friends are ready to sympathise: 'Don't worry – you'll do better next time.' But in truth you, and perhaps they too, know that 'next time' is a long way off, if it ever arrives at all.

But don't give up, don't stop trying to cope with your problems. It's amazing, when you determine to overcome a lifelong fear, how simple action and commitment strengthen your resolve and develop your confidence. And in the process your perceived fear fades into insignificance.

Failure can be an experience you identify with, or it can be a lesson you learn from. The choice is yours, and it will determine whether you see yourself as a loser or as a winner.

If you want to succeed, focus clearly on the outcome of the success you're striving for. Don't let the memory of past setbacks create mental blocks. Apply your mind and your skills to what you are doing. Banish all thoughts of failure.

There is always another way of doing something; don't *assume* the solution is going to be hard to find, and don't overlook the obvious. Before you decide to give up on the apparently locked door, check the handle.

A small boy who loved baseball was given a new bat as a birthday present. Excitedly he dashed outside, shouting, 'I'm the best batter in the whole world!' He threw his ball high in the air, swung the bat and missed. Undeterred, he picked the ball up a second time and yelled defiantly, 'I'm the best batter in the world!' This time he threw the ball much higher, kept his eye on it and took a bigger swing – but again he missed, pirouetting before falling to the ground. Now he was a bit bruised, but all the same he stood up a third time, threw the ball even higher and took the biggest swing ever. This time he missed so completely that he lost hold of the bat and crashed to the ground so heavily that he grazed both knees. He sat up, looked at the bat, looked at the ball, then shouted excitedly, 'Hey, what do you know? I'm the greatest pitcher in the world!'

When your self-belief is based on truth, the world will believe in you

You have to create a winning outlook and a strong self-belief; you have to turn those negative statements into positive statements. When you think to yourself, 'I am getting old,' see it in a positive light – you have a lot of experience and wisdom. Instead of thinking, 'I'm not smart enough,' say to yourself instead, 'I get on well with people, I'm enthusiastic about what I'm doing and I'm reliable.'

When you look at the lives of people you admire, don't imagine yourself as being so very different from them. Don't think it was easy for them – it wasn't. They will have had more or less the same number of hardships and setbacks that you will probably encounter. They didn't all have some kind of extraordinary natural talent, but what they did have was an extraordinary natural belief in the talent they did have. And though they may have been unique in the way they ran their lives or set up their businesses, you too are unique. If you had the opportunity to meet one of your heroes, which of your qualities would you want them to admire?

Never give in – never, never, never give in.

Winston Churchill (1874–1965)

We've said before that successful people are individuals who get up one time more than they fall down. When you feel good about yourself, you take hiccups and even substantial obstacles in your stride. It's as though you are in harmony with the universe itself; nothing is a problem. But never lose sight of the fact that you *do* have a choice in how you feel about the hardships you encounter. And the choices you make will determine whether you persevere or whether you give up. By continuing to persevere you create a 'can do' image of yourself that becomes fixed in your subconscious; you develop a new set of behaviours and habits congruent with this new image of yourself. This new set of behaviours and habits empowers you to endure and overcome the hardships that you may experience in the future.

Great works are performed not by strength but by perseverance.

Samuel Johnson (1709–1784)

When those who have succeeded in business talk of their early hardships and difficulties, they do not speak of experiences they wish they never had. They talk of lessons learned, of character-building experiences that made them the people they are. And what they all had in common was the ability to persevere, to go through fear of failure and come out the other side.

You can cover any distance, no matter how far, if you are prepared to persevere. Perseverance is not about pursuing the impossible – that is stupidity. A saying often attributed to Albert Einstein reveals the difference between genius and stupidity: 'I have learned in life that there is a limit to genius!' Perseverance is not exclusive to extraordinary individuals who have demonstrated superhuman feats of endurance; it is simply the determined resolve to work towards your chosen goal, come what may.

In a letter to his young son, G. Kingsley Ward, a Canadian businessman wrote, 'No one I know has ever experienced a life without defeats, failures, disappointments and frustrations galore along the way; learning to overcome these times of agony is what separates the winners from the losers.'

FOCUS ON THE PRIZE, NOT THE PROBLEM

When a setback occurs it's too easy to focus our energy on the injustice, the unfairness of it or simply be distracted by it. We should use that same focus and energy to find a solution, and move forward.

In 1961, John F. Kennedy declared his ambitious dream that America would put a man on the moon within the next ten years. It was a perfect example of what we said earlier: identify the where and the when and then you will find the how. At that time, the idea of being able to create the systems necessary to take three men to the moon, land and bring them back, belonged in the realms of science fiction and yet on 20th July 1969, Neil Armstrong stepped onto the lunar surface. How was so much achieved so quickly? The fact is that the whole space race was driven by the Cold War, each nation competing with the other and seeking to demonstrate to the world its superior technology. It was this that concentrated the Americans on their goal, made them focus on the prize and enabled them to overcome the countless problems that arose.

Obstacles are those frightful things you see when you take your eyes off your goal.

Henry Ford (1863–1947)

Focusing on the prize does not guarantee success, but it makes the journey towards it purposeful and confidence-building. The principal reason, I believe, why many people fail is because they lose sight of their initial dream. Their initial enthusiasm wanes because they start to focus on the consequences of failure. I have often met individuals who talk passionately to me about the business they are planning to start. They are going to leave their safe employment in three months' time and go it alone. But as the starting date draws closer, they tell you more and more about the problems they are facing. These difficulties are no doubt real, but what's actually happening is that the fear factor has magnified and the consequences of imagined failure have become almost too awful to contemplate. And so, increasingly, whether they admit it or not, they've become paralysed into inaction, and this inaction reinforces the expectation of the imagined failure until it becomes a reality.

> Do something! Take action. Outcomes will follow, the outcomes become our guides

Identify problems within your plan and let your subconscious mind solve them for you.

The answer will often appear as a flash of inspiration, or a moment of recognition. Remember, when you put a problem into your subconscious, it will work on it until it finds a solution. This solution will appear as though from nowhere. (For a more detailed explanation see Appendix Your Brain pages 262-282.)

Visualise yourself in your new company or office and the rewards you will reap. When the going gets tough return to these powerful images of future success. Once you have reached your goal, the journey you had to make to get there never seems so tough, because success has brought with it the habit of remembering strong positive memories of the experience, which your brain will now automatically store for use when you have to face future challenges.

The brain can be conditioned to focus on the positive and avoid remembering the negative. A sprinter focuses on the tape and on coming first. He doesn't focus on the opposition, because that would undermine his concentration. A racing driver succinctly expressed it when asked why he had not crashed by saying, 'I only concentrate on where I want to go.'

What happens when you have positive focus, pure and simple? Here's an example from my chosen sport – yes, golf again. It's an absolute joy to watch a young child putt for the first time. Children seem to have the most natural swings. Give them a four- or five-foot putt and they look at the hole, look at the ball, then swing the club and sink the putt – just as well as, if not better than, many an experienced golfer. They are complete naturals, utterly uninhibited by the fear of failure; they have no problems to focus on. They don't understand the mechanics of the golf swing or of the putting stroke; their minds are completely clear of negative thoughts or memories – of the junk that adults carry around with them. For children, putting is the most natural and easiest thing in the world.

As we grow older, though, we concentrate less on the desired outcome and more on the difficulties of getting there, trying to control things that are best left to the subconscious. And as long as you are preoccupied with problems you magnify them in your mind. As a golfer, you start hooding the blade, swinging across the line, lifting your head up, shortening your backswing – any or all of these in an attempt consciously to do it right.

So, when you close in on your target, whatever it may be, try to do so with the uncluttered and fearless approach of the child.

CREATIVE PROBLEM-SOLVING

When we have a problem to solve we almost always resort to the same old habit of thinking, and so it's hardly surprising that we come up with the same old solution. The same old solution may well be no solution at all to the issue at hand. What we have to do is develop a way of solving our problems creatively, allowing our imagination to play its natural role.

When you do a crossword puzzle you tend to follow a pattern of thought, but faced with other problems, falling into familiar pattern often limits your ability to solve. Someone once said to me, 'If you want one solution to a problem ask an expert, but if you want a hundred ask an idiot.'

We all tend to operate within the limits of our known abilities, instead of venturing outside them. Often people say, 'I'm not creative, I'm practical. I'm good with my hands but I'm not creative.' Put that to one side, do not be limited by a belief in your lack of imagination. Remember this above all else: ideas are currency. Every project, every achievement, began as a creative spark in somebody's imagination.

You have an imagination that is capable of creating your solutions, so use it.

Ideas are like rabbits. You get a couple and learn how to handle them, and pretty soon you have a dozen.

John Steinbeck (1902–1968)

How do you go about doing this? Start by writing the problem down – this will help you to define clearly what it is, to see clearly the parameters. Then, once you've identified the problem, write down as many ways of solving it as you can think of. They can be as far-fetched as you like – just let your mind empty itself of possible solutions, then leave it for a while. When you return to it a bit later your subconscious will have continued working on the difficulty; come back to it after several hours or even a day or two, and you'll be surprised at how quickly answers start to appear. Allowing your mind a free rein in this way will help to break the mould of your current habits of thought.

If you want a ten-mile-an-hour increase in train speed, you tinker with horsepower – double its speed, and you have to break out of conventional performance expectations.

Jack Welch (b. 1935)

Everything created was first imagined

Ideas can come from anywhere. Whatever business you are in, you are first and foremost in the ideas business. When I worked as a television producer in an entertainment development unit, our job was to look for and generate fresh ideas for television from a variety of sources ranging from foreign broadcasters to members of the public. I must have read close on 4,000 programme proposals in my three years there, and the fact is I never saw a bad one. Certainly there were proposals which were so off the wall as to have no feasible place on a television schedule, but I always felt it was my responsibility to encourage anybody who wrote in.

The strangest proposal I received was for a programme based on boxing and draughts. The man's idea was that two amateur boxers would box for three minutes, then play speed draughts for three minutes. The first person to submit or to lose at draughts was out! I remember my letter back: thanks for submitting the idea, but it wouldn't fit in to our current scheduling plans nor would it attract a large audience, but if he had any other proposals that I would be happy to receive them.

The man did in fact write to me again, and though I couldn't take any of his ideas forward, I always hoped my replies would encourage him to send me more – because, as I said earlier, there is no such thing as a good idea or a bad idea: there are simply ideas that can or that cannot be applied to a particular issue or at a particular time. I believed it was always possible that he might come up with an idea which could be a great entertainment show and a ratings winner. Every idea has to come from somewhere – why not him?

It's rather like knowledge: it isn't power in itself – it's only applied knowledge that constitutes power. Telling someone that their ideas are no good will stop them being creative and deprive you of possible solutions to future problems.

The creative process is one we all have admission to. Ideas are currency: how much money is in *your* creative bank at the moment?

Being open to ideas from all sources pays enormous dividends. This is clearly demonstrated in the case of Toyota, whose 47,000 employees in Japan generated 1.8 million suggestions in 1990. Companies that invite their staff to be involved in the creation of ideas that will impact on the business, or to identify problems and suggest solutions, benefit from a highly motivated, appreciative and loyal workforce – and some great ideas

The deepest principle of human nature is the craving to be appreciated

William James (1842–1910)

Little things can make a big difference. Little suggestions can make the difference between things working and not working. Be open to your ability to solve your problems creatively. And when you're stumped, ask others what they would do, how they would approach whatever it is that's impeding your progress.

> When I was making television shows in small regional stations, I used to delight in watching the engineers solve unanticipated production difficulties. Never once did they say whatever it was couldn't be done. They would often go off for a while, then re-appear with some contraption they had designed on the spot to create just the effect we needed.
>
> As Scotty in *Star Trek* used to say, 'It's a long shot, Captain, but it might just work.' Trust your intuition, trust your long shots: they might just work.

THERE'S ALWAYS ANOTHER WAY

No matter how bleak things may appear, no matter how seemingly intractable the problem, never give up, never give in. There is *always* another way to skin that rabbit. To put it another way, when you feel you've reached the bottom – dig a little deeper. What have you got to lose? Never live in fear that there is no solution. Never believe there is nothing to be done. You may need encouragement and practical help – but there is *always* a way through.

During the Second World War many prisoners were interned in prisoner-of-war camps. What resources did they have? Very few and yet by working together sharing knowledge they were able to devise many ingenious ways of overcoming seemingly insurmountable odds and escaping: by digging tunnels with home made tools, or cobbling together elaborate disguises. They found a way.

See creative problem-solving as a tool. Have absolute faith in your ability and in the ability of friends and colleagues; be ready to exploit all the resources you can lay your hands on. In a study of self-made millionaires the researcher concluded that there were two key qualities common to the subjects: one was that they believed that there was always a way, a solution to any problem and the other was that they prioritised only working on those things that truly mattered at the time.

Prioritising is the key to using your time effectively, and later we'll look at a simple way of creating daily, weekly and monthly priority lists. But the point to grasp now is that *there is always a solution*. Remember, many of the world's most important discoveries and achievements were made only after everything else had been tried – because people refused to give up.

But don't feel you should be looking for solutions only when things are not working. Start by seeking to improve your *modus operandi* when things are going well. Some people say, 'If it ain't broke, don't fix it,' and I agree with them. But I also think that, whatever your working methods, you should consistently seek to improve them.

Commercial history is full of innovators whose ideas were ridiculed and ignored at the time only to come up trumps later. The creative process is all about respect for knowledge, and especially for imagination. Problems are puzzles to be solved, not handicaps to pull us down. Never ridicule anyone's ideas – that's too easy to do and not in anyone's interest. If you don't like, a particular suggestion, say something like 'I don't think this will work for me at the moment', but encourage the individual whose suggestion it is because one day he or she may come up with the gem that turns your life around.

It was rarely the case, I imagine, that the great inventors of the twentieth century woke up one morning with the exact solution to a problem complete in their minds. Trial and error were what brought their ideas to fruition. So when your plan is failing to get you to your destination, what do you do? Do you change your plan or do you change your destination? Winners change their plan, fearlessly, with the confidence that they can do it; their destination remains the same.

REMEMBER

- Failure is a learning experience of the moment – learn the lesson
- Most fear is based on imagined outcomes – that have not happened!
- Face your fears – see them as illusions in your mind – and they will disappear

9

COMMITMENT

COMMITMENT IS
CONTINUING TO DO
THE THING YOU
DETERMINED TO DO
LONG AFTER YOUR
ENTHUSIASM HAS DIED

Unless commitment is made, there are only promises and hopes . . .

Peter Drucker (b. 1909)

Age is unrelated to people's commitment to their job and their level of job performance.

Tuuli and Karisalmi, 1999. 'Impact of Working Life Quality on Burnout', *Experimental Ageing Research*, vol. 25, pp. 441–49

COMMITMENT

Do people fail because they are unlucky and therefore the victims of forces beyond their influence? Is it possible that some successes are just not destined to be? I don't know what you believe. I do know that in order to realise your goal, to create your success, it is important that you demonstrate commitment.

Many people understand the notion of commitment within an emotional relationship; yet some would say commitment in a relationship is something we have no control over. You either are – or are not. In reality you choose to be committed to a relationship. The idea that it is something that you have no control over is wishful thinking. It is my belief that commitment is a choice. It is a choice over which we have 100 per cent control. We can commit to a diet, to getting healthy, to working longer. We can commit to studying, we can commit to giving 100 per cent of our ability, we can commit to a relationship – or we can choose not to.

> In winners, commitment is what remains behind after enthusiasm has died in others

In theory, commitment to our goal should be easy because we want it. In practice it is very hard, because when our plans get knocked off course, or when we experience a setback, there is a small persistent voice from within that says, 'I knew you'd fail, you always do'. This failure, rather than being merely an upset and increasing our resolve and desire to succeed – tends to reinforce a deeply held personal belief that we never were going to succeed anyway. For that reason it is essential when you revisit your goal and when you revisit your plan, every day, that you must also revisit your commitment. The form this takes can be varied. It may be a personal pledge spoken aloud every morning. It may be sticking to an absolutely predetermined regime of exercise or a timetable of events irrespective of the fact they're not immediately working. Does this sound too obvious? I guess not, because commitment is usually the first principle to fail when a goal is given up on. When a goal is abandoned and you want to find the reason it was abandoned, people will say it was unrealistic. It was a stretch too far, it wasn't what they really wanted. But if you examine and scratch deeply enough you'll find that the commitment wasn't there or the commitment wasn't strong enough.

> Desire is the key to motivation, but it's determination and commitment to an unrelenting pursuit of your goal – a commitment to excellence – that will enable you to attain the success you seek.
>
> *Mario Andretti* (b. 1940)

Imagine your friend is going to sing in public. Now this is no ordinary friend, it is absolutely your best friend in the world, your number one buddy in your life, who you've known since childhood. With whom you've shared ups and downs, highs and lows, emotional traumas and the greatest successes of life. You love this person. However, he's has been asked to sing in public and he's agreed. You happen to also know that he is very shy, but he loves to sing and is, in fact, very gifted. He's been invited to a small recital in a local concert hall. He asks you to be there for him. He asks you to sit in the front row and give him a friendly face to look out to. You promise him that come hell or high water, you'll be there. You know that he's going to concentrate on his nerves, he's going to concentrate on his fear of singing in public. You, on the other hand, will be concentrating on his enjoying the experience and being successful. You know how important it is to be there for him, sitting in the front row. So here's the big question: would you let him down?

No. I didn't think you would.

Why wouldn't you let him down? Because you would honour your promise. Because you love him and you want to share that moment with him. You wouldn't dream of letting him down. So why do so many people let themselves down? Why do we give up on our goals? Why do you give up on your goals? Think about it. In the run up to your friend's concert, imagine he started expressing doubt, getting cold feet and focusing on the negatives. What would you do? Would you reinforce those beliefs or would you encourage your friend to concentrate on a more powerful outcome, a positive outcome, to believe in it being a success? I think you would encourage him with all your heart. You would reinforce your belief in him and hopefully his belief in himself, and you would do this not because it is important that he sings well on the night, but because it is important to you that he believes in himself and in his dreams. You would do it because *you care*, and yet here is the sad news. Most people who fail don't care about themselves or their goal enough to stay committed so they just give up.

I have seen that high achievers, those who succeed in the realisation of their goals, have this ability to remain committed to their goal just by sticking to it. They continue to focus on the goal long after the initial enthusiasm for what they are seeking has passed.

So how do you make yourself committed? You must both believe in the goal and understand that the goal alone is not enough and never has been. The world is full of people with unfulfilled ambitions. To succeed you must renew your commitment every day – if this seems too often, trust me it isn't. If you do it as often as you can, it will reinforce in your mind the need to give 100 per cent of your effort irrespective of the experiences along the way that may give you a temporary setback. Wouldn't it be great if somehow we could just make a commitment to ourselves and persist in the realisation of our goals by not letting ourselves down? You can – if you choose to. So get rid of your Book of Excuses, you don't need it anymore.

STAYING THE COURSE

I am often asked, what is one of the most common characteristics of successful people, and the answer in truth, is their ability never to give up. It is their ability to persist. And unless you are committed to an outcome, you will not persist. These high achievers see setbacks as opportunities to learn. They do not identify with failure, they use it as a feedback mechanism from which to move on. They have learned to stay committed to the course.

So how do we commit to staying the course? I have no doubt that many of you reading this would like to know the answer. Is it really possible? I say this because it is likely that you have a history of giving up – most of us do, otherwise we'd all be super successful. Most of us have a history of giving up and a strong memory of not seeing our goals through, so let's start with the bad news: every time you give up, you reinforce a stronger emotional memory of failure. That is so important in understanding why we fail. In fact it gets to the point – and I'm absolutely serious about this, and I have no doubt that when you read it you will think, yeah I agree with that but it doesn't apply to me – it gets to the point that when we give up, we not only feel relieved, we justify the failure and don't feel bad about it at all, in fact in some cases we actually feel good.

Here, are three thoughts which I believe, are very important in understanding commitment:

1 I believe we can fake commitment to other people for just a little while, but we cannot fake it to ourselves, even for a moment.
2 True commitment is reinforced by a strong sense of personal responsibility to ourselves and others.

3 The reason we don't commit is because we are afraid we will fail. If we commit and fail then we believe our self-image or self-esteem will be crushed.

I use the word crushed because people believe they will be devastated and will be failures for the rest of their lives. That is negative thinking at its most damaging. Trust me, you won't be crushed. You will either give up (I hope not) or you will learn, become stronger in the process, deal with it and carry on.

But, you may be thinking, what if you are committed – and I mean truly committed? You are giving 110 per cent, seven days a week, and still things don't work out. Now what? That's the easy one, you reassess your plan and you start again. Commitment isn't an action, commitment isn't a behaviour, commitment is an *attitude in action*. And once that attitude is in place, the behaviour and the action will follow.

Weakness of attitude becomes weakness of character.

Albert Einstein (1879–1955)

We saw earlier that research indicates that some 80 per cent of the skills we require to enable us to succeed in life or in business or in relationships, are in fact attitudes. Attitude-based skills. These can be compassion, understanding, listening, focus, attention, concentration. The other 20 per cent will be actual skills, not attitudes, but if you draw up a list of them for yourself, you'll generally find that 80 per cent of the skills we require are attitude-based. What follows then is the understanding that you control your attitude, that *you* choose it. It's mind-boggling. The ability to read, to write, to drive a car or to play the violin, these are skills. They are skills which no amount of positive attitude in the world will make up for. Imagine, reading one positive attitude book or one positive thinking book too many and as a result of which you enter a violin music contest.

You bluff you're way in because, by golly, you've got more positive attitude and self-belief than a cheerleaders' convention. With that winning way and the daily dose of positive reinforcement you administer with a wink to yourself in the mirror every morning, you stride onto the stage, grasping a violin you bought some hours earlier. You give the audience that confident smile that you've been practising for hours in front of the mirror, which surprises the audience as most of the contestants up to this point have looked pretty serious, nervous and somewhat focused. This magnificent stranger that no one has ever heard of strides on to stage with purpose, commitment, confidence in spades and a winning attitude. There's only one problem – no amount of self-belief and positive attitude will help you if you have little or no knowledge to apply.

Attitude is a little thing that makes a big difference.

Winston Churchill (1874–1965)

Well, you get the drift don't you? You accelerate your performance levels greatly when the skills are driven by attitude. Commitment doesn't require any ability. It doesn't require a mechanical or a knowledge-based skill. Now isn't that great news? Isn't that simply one of the most enlightening, uplifting bits of information you could have? Commitment, doesn't require ability, it requires an inner belief, an inner determination to stay the course. Because it means, as with all attitudes, that you can choose it. You can choose it right here, right now. Commitment is an attitude, not a skill.

> Commitment doesn't require any ability other than determination – which is an attitude

Would you give up on a diet if you didn't see visible results in five minutes? Obviously that's stupid, that's too short, so let's say five days? That might be too long, so how about five hours? No! Five hours is not a good time because we could all agree that there would be no visible difference. Yet many people don't make it to day five of the diet, because it's just too damn hard, and yet five days is simply made up of twenty-four consecutive five-hour periods. Which is why we must renew our commitment to the goal every day, so we never allow ourselves off the hook and justify giving up.

Commitment requires a high degree of confidence to be truly effective. Remember that confidence comes from the Latin words *cum fides*, meaning 'with faith'. True confidence is faith in ourselves. It requires that we ignore our past negative behaviours, that we accept them and learn from them as part of who we were, and determine not to repeat them again. This is difficult because our memory of past failures is much more strongly imprinted on our subconscious, with its associated emotions, than our past memories of success. That means that when we think of the goal, we automatically remember our past failures, and the pain or shame we associate with them. Therefore I use the word faith appropriately for faith to me is a belief in something for which there is no empirical evidence – only a conviction, a belief in the object of our faith, whatever it may be. And that faith is enabled through our commitment. When you believe you can, you will.

History is full of individuals who have been committed to a cause. Despite major obstacles, Reihold Messner was the first man to ascend Mount Everest without oxygen, before he went on to set other mountaineering records that will probably never be equalled. Alex Dyson, the inventor of the bagless vacuum cleaner, had to re-mortgage his house and faced bankruptcy on a number of occasions, but he never gave up on his dream. Now he is worth hundreds of millions of pounds.

I once met a single mother in Glasgow, when I was working as a door-to-door salesman. I was in a poor part of town and sold gadgets through hire purchase. I didn't realise at the time, but, as with so many of these products which are dressed up to look expensive and cutting edge in technology, they were badly made, overpriced items designed to get people into a money trap through a borrowing scheme (I am much wiser now).

Failure will never overtake me if my determination to succeed is strong enough.

Og Mandino (1923–1996)

Whilst giving a demonstration, she listened and kindly made me a cup of tea. I asked her how long she'd lived there. Twenty-five years she said, adding that she'd brought up three children. She showed me their graduation photographs: they were all doctors, she'd put them through university, made them stay the course, committed her life to helping them realise their goals. There are just so many examples of committed individuals and I suggest that you immerse yourself in their life stories. Listen to them, read about them and be inspired by them, because you too have a unique journey in life and commitment is going to make all the difference.

Enthusiasm is no substitute for commitment

A word of caution though. Enthusiasm as I mentioned earlier, is, cheap and cheerful. It's abundant, easy to fake and hard to ignore – but never in the history of mankind has it got anything done. It is a powerful, positive feeling but without commitment, it fades away. Don't confuse a feeling of enthusiasm for an indicator of outcome. Enthusiasm cannot sustain itself without reinforcement, encouragement and results – or if it does, then chances are, it is delusional.

Commitment by contrast is not a behaviour; it is an attitude. You cannot teach people to be committed. You can get them to understand its importance, but it is they and they alone who must make the commitment. Without a personal desire to see things through, to do what it takes, to walk the extra mile, no amount of talk in the world will make any difference.

KEEP IT PERSONAL

At a personal level, commitment and purpose are very, very closely linked. And from purpose comes passion, that marvellous invisible quality that comes from the heart. It enables us to never give up, to stay the course to make that final phone call, to ask for the business, or for someone's hand in marriage. It comes from within this wonderful quality and it is critical to success, along with commitment and purpose.

I hitchhiked from Glasgow down to London when I was at college and late one night I got a lift with an elderly fellow. It was a Wednesday, and he was on his way to London to watch a second division football club. When I asked him how long he had been supporting this club he said, for most of his life. It was wet and dark and I asked him how far away he lived. About 80 miles from the ground he replied. I said he must be a true fan to drive all this way in the rain, to see them and he told me that it wasn't the first team, it was the reserve team. He didn't follow the main team, but their second team he supported passionately. He never missed a game, home or indeed away if he got the chance, and in my naivety as a young man who probably should have shown slightly more respect, I said, 'You mean to tell me that you're happy to get in the car, drive 80 miles down the M1, then across London to the other side of town, in the rain to watch the reserves play. How many people would watch the match?"

'Oh sometimes we get up to 40 or 50 people watching,' I said incredulously.

'You like that?'

He paused and looked at me equally incredulously and he said, 'I love it.'

Passion and commitment, hand in hand.

At school most of us probably did not blindly follow our headmaster. Chances are that the only time we saw him was in his study for disciplinary reasons, or perhaps at the morning assembly. But chances are also that there was one teacher (I sincerely hope there was anyway) who you liked more than all the others. Who inspired you, whom you trusted and would respect and follow? Why was this? Why did this person have such a profound effect on us – that we absolutely believed in them? I think the reasons are quite simple: they were enthusiastic, passionate about the subject they taught and about bringing it to life for you. When you got something right they praised you and when you got something wrong they were still encouraging. They made you feel good about yourself. They were committed and passionate about developing your potential, about changing your life – and they did. That's why you remember them.

> Take full responsibility for how you make the people you meet feel

For our personal journey to our success, commitment is absolutely imperative. We need to commit 100 per cent to staying the course that will guide us to our goal, though we may change our plan as necessary. But a word of caution: it is hard, it can be lonely, and with the best intentions in the world we can fall over, sometimes more often than we would have believed possible. It is easy to give up – in fact, giving up is easier than falling off a log, because to fall off a log you have to climb up on it in the first place. To give up you just have to say the words 'I quit.' It would be great if there was a magic pill that would give you 24 hours of absolute commitment –

you could take one every day. Sadly of course there isn't and there never will be. Why? Because the ingredients simply don't exist in the physical world.

I have good news though: there is hope. There is an opportunity to shape our destiny and give ourselves our greatest chance of happiness. That opportunity comes in the form of personal choice. We can choose to take the responsibility of being and staying committed – but before we go any further I want you to agree one thing. That is, that you commit with passion, because when you're passionate about your goal, then commitment is easy, it's automatic and effortless. But without passion, staying committed is not just hard, it is not just really hard – it's impossible.

We frequently associate passion with love and romance where it can make us do crazy things. It's a powerful thing. In business, if you are passionate about the goal you are aiming for then all aspects of the challenge – winning, being loyal to your colleagues, making a difference, being significant, creating value – are greatly enhanced. At an individual personal level, commitment will frequently be tested and probably more often than not we will fail in the first couple of hurdles. That's where passion comes in. Without it we'll fail the test – it will be over. But if you get back on track and try again and again, in a true reflection of your passion and commitment, then I know that after your last failure will come success. Success is so much about our willingness to persist irrespective of the setbacks and humiliations we suffer, because to persist in the realisation of an ideal is proof of commitment. It is all too easy in life to quit, to protest, that you were truly committed, that you really persisted and persisted but then, you failed, I just don't believe that's they way it is. I believe you truly fail in life only when you quit. Up until that point there is always the possibility that you will succeed, but when your commitment fails and you give up, then it's impossible.

> Don't quit on yourself and your dreams – not ever

You and no one else in the world is responsible for your level of commitment. Accept that responsibility. Commitment is an attitude: you alone choose it. So choose it, and use it.

REMEMBER

- Commitment is doing the thing you said you would do – long after your desire to do it has passed
- Most people fail because they quit – never give up
- Sticking to it is the hard part – renew your commitment to the goal every day until it is realised

10

CELEBRATION

WE CELEBRATE THINGS
NOT TO MAKE US
HAPPY, BUT BECAUSE WE
ARE HAPPY, AND EACH
TIME WE DO SO, WE SEE
OURSELVES IN A MORE
POSITIVE LIGHT

There are high spots in all of our lives and most of them have come about through encouragement from someone else. I don't care how great, how famous or successful a man or woman may be, each hungers for applause.

George M. Adams (1837–1920)

Researchers find that an optimistic personal outlook is more than just seeing the bright side of things. Believing in yourself actually produces increases in good health, motivation, and achievement in 60 per cent of people.

Schulman, P. 1999. 'Applying Learned Optimism to Increase Sales Productivity', *Journal of Personal Selling and Sales Management*, vol. 19, pp. 31–37

CELEBRATION

There are people who ask, why celebrate anything? What good does it do? There's no scientific proof to show that it increases productivity or affects economic growth, so what's the point? But the answer to their question – apart from the fact that it is just plain, feel-good fun – is that celebration addresses what research has shown to be the two key factors in personal motivation: the need to be appreciated and the desire to be involved.

As children we received a great deal of praise in our development, and it made us feel good about ourselves. We still respond to praise and seek it from our peer group, as we sought it out from our teachers and our parents. We want to be told that we're clever, we're good, we're not naughty; we want to be told that we are succeeding in the expectations of others.

> The self-image of a child at the age of ten is a greater predictor of their future success in life than their IQ

That self-image is based upon feedback from the world at large. And whenever we succeed in achieving something of value or significance, however small, praise, appreciation or celebration will help reinforce our sense of success, and our positive self-image, in our subconscious.

Correction does much, but encouragement does more.

Johann Wolfgang von Goethe (1749–1832)

When I was eleven, an Italian priest who had some students in his care invited me to go skiing with them one day. We travelled in a mini-bus up to Glencoe where we hired the very elementary ski equipment (this was Scotland in 1967). Then we set off up the slopes with the abandonment of the foolish or the ignorant. The priest had a little skiing experience, as did one or two of the students, but most of us were first timers. Leather boots were strapped onto feet, and then in turn attached to skis; corduroy trousers and thick woollen jumpers were the order of the day. There was not a great deal of snow – earth and rocks were showing through – but eventually we found a patch of snow that was wide enough and long enough for us to try our hand at the grand alpine sport of skiing. I fell over many, many times but each time I was encouraged to try again, and whenever I did something that remotely resembled skiing I would get a, 'Well done Robin, keep going – you're doing very well.' He continually encouraged me to believe I was a good skier.

Well, it was another fifteen years before I actually went onto a proper ski slope, and of course I had to start again from scratch. But I'd always remembered fondly that first day on the slopes and when, all those years later, they asked if I could ski, I said, 'Yes, I've skied in Scotland.'

About four years ago, when I was moving house, I came across an old storage box, containing stuff from my younger years. A photograph fell out of a book: it was obviously taken that day in the Scottish mountains Written in block capitals were the words 'KEEP GOING!!' with two exclamation marks, and then the name of the priest signed below, Father Bertone. Seeing that picture brought back to me all the strong memories of the day, and now I have it framed on my desk, and whenever I'm feeling just a little bit overwhelmed by life, I look at it and remember to keep going. Father Bertone's kind words of encouragement and his celebration of my smallest successes have stayed with me to this day.

Most of us, swimming against the tides of trouble the world knows nothing about, need only a bit of praise or encouragement – and we will make the goal.

Robert Collier (1885–1950)

It seems very natural that we all celebrate birthdays, Christmas or other festivals. Yet isn't it strange that we need an excuse to celebrate or that it has to follow a certain form. We might not send cards except for birthdays, at Christmas or as thank you notes – but we're equally able to celebrate achievement through the simple act of praise by saying, 'Well done'. Celebration doesn't need fireworks or champagne; we can let others know that we are thinking of them, or that we appreciate their efforts, by a phone call or an email. We don't stop needing this praise just because we are adults. When children behave in ways we wish to reinforce, we use phrases like, 'Good boy' and 'Good girl,' to make them aware we are pleased and approving. It's the same with dogs: we teach them with rewards and praise, with enthusiastic patting of the back or scratching of the head to reinforce correct behaviour.

We celebrate their doing something right. Sure it's behavioural, but when we do it, we see them – children and dogs – grow in confidence and quickly develop the skills we're encouraging. As adults, our welcome response to such praise never changes and yet it seems as if one day, sadly, unconditional praise and positive reinforcement just stop. We get to an age where we're simply meant to get on with it. I suspect it is assumed that as we are no longer helpless children, we should have reached an age of reason in which celebration is no longer necessary. But it is necessary. We all need appreciation and the motivation it affords. When we celebrate success, we create in ourselves a strong emotional identification with success, a memory that's stored away for future use.

True happiness is . . . to enjoy the present, without anxious dependence upon the future.

Seneca (c. 4 BC–65 AD)

And recalling it makes us identify with a feeling of well-being and confidence.

As you may have gathered by now I am a very keen golfer. I've played since the age of four and travelled to some of the most exciting, remote, difficult and downright dangerous courses in the world in pursuit of the game I love so much. I had a chance meeting one day on the old course at St Andrews with two wonderful Americans who introduced themselves as Bosch and Nemo, and as the years passed we stayed in touch and became friends. Every year we would get together and have a match. Over time the match grew is scale until it became a formal fixture of eight players a side, a four-day competition of match play, every bit as dramatic as the Ryder Cup, but much more exciting (or at least so it felt). One year I was playing in Michigan on the final day in a game we just had to win to have any chance of taking the series. I was partnered by my friend Neil against two Americans whom we were immensely keen to beat. It had been a very demanding match, we came to the 15th green, we were down and things were looking bad. I had a 60-foot putt (well, perhaps a bit less but it grows longer in the telling). It was uphill with an eight inch break to the left, and I had to sink it otherwise the game would be over. I've never felt in my life so determined to sink a putt. My feelings at the time were of immense confidence. I looked at Neil and I said, 'Don't worry, I'm going to sink the putt.' (Admittedly not the most inspiring of quotes but I had no idea I was going to be reliving the next twenty seconds so often throughout my life).

I stepped up to the shot, stood for what seemed like an age, then I struck it firmly and stepped back. Even when it was only ten feet away from my putter, with another 50 feet to travel, I knew it was going in. It ran true and straight and at the end it took the break of eight inches and dropped dead centre. I jumped off the ground in joy. Neil ran and hugged me. The Americans were stunned. That simple putt and the celebration that followed it are as deeply burned into my psyche as any experience I've had. And faced with times of challenge, I can think of that putt and recall the feeling.

Winning isn't everything. Wanting to win is.

Jim 'Catfish' Hunter (1946–1999)

Watch a football team play, see what happens when one of them scores a goal – his team mates run up to him and they hug, they punch the air, they celebrate, they do somersaults, they pull their shirts over their heads, they run to the crowd and dance every dance known to mankind except for the military two-step; they are just ecstatic. It's a release of deep felt joy and a way of reinforcing the moment. Which is why no one in the team runs up to the goal scorer and says, 'Well, that's what we pay you for.'

> Celebrate your success, and you will create moments. Moments are what your life is all about

To reinforce and grow a strong self-image of yourself as succeeding, *celebrate every goal* that you achieve along the way. No matter how small, no matter if you just say to yourself, 'Wow' and feel genuinely good about it. Are there any better words of encouragement in the world than, 'Well done'? In the absence of a cheerleader, become your own cheerleader.

As we grow as unique persons, we learn to respect the uniqueness of others.

Robert H. Schuller (b. 1926)

'You are the most unique person in the history of the world'. I hope you understand this and believe it. No one like you has ever existed before, you have unique gifts, insights and purpose. Never for one moment stop believing that you make a huge difference both to the world at large, and the world at hand. I don't mean that you are uniquely special in some self-inflated egotistical way; this is not about self-glorification or being important. I have very little time for people who claim a positive attitude is all that's needed for everything else to be fine. That may be a great sentiment but it's potentially dangerous advice, because I think if we allow ourselves to be blinded to the reality of life, we can easily delude ourselves and, dangerously, we can delude others.

Rather, I want us to celebrate our unique successes in life, every step of the way, even if only with a gentle moment of self-appreciation, a quietly spoken well done. I once ran a marathon ill-prepared – the New York Marathon – for charity. I remember very vividly six miles into the race, as I was jogging along saying to myself, 'Well done mate, you're really doing it.' I had a lump in my throat, and my eyes were filling up with tears. I had reconnected with a deep emotional part of myself with which I had lost contact – to the person who would, as my mother had said many years before, always complete any job he put his mind to. So why was I was celebrating and praising myself? I was reinforcing the fact that I was on track with my goal. I was in the process of realising a goal. It created a very powerful emotional response in me (and I have to admit I'm kind of an emotional person). I felt great. The crowd was cheering and I finished the race.

I remember afterwards how sore my legs were, and I had to make my way back to the apartment I was staying in. I wandered around and eventually found a subway. It was very busy, and when I got onto the train there was only one seat free. I went for it at the same time that a young lady did and, although we arrived simultaneously, I said, 'There you go, you can have the seat.'

She sat down and said thank you and then she looked up at me. Seeing my tracksuit and my exhausted expression, she asked, 'Have you just run the Marathon?'

'Yup, I have,' I said.

And she stood up, saying with a smile, 'Well, you deserve this seat, good for you.'

Another small celebration.

I sincerely believe that the deepest need of the individual is to be loved unconditionally. We need to feel valued and validated in the world in which we live, to be respected and to be able to respect others; and it is those needs which can motivate us to do the extraordinary. Monitor how you feel. Do your actions make you feel good? If you do something that makes you feel bad, determine not to do it again. Don't justify your failures, and pretend everything's okay. But do celebrate events or outcomes that make you feel good, and you will seriously help develop a winning self-image.

There are two things people want more than sex and money . . . recognition and praise.

Mary Kay Ash (1918–2001)

In the workplace, naturally, financial incentives are very important and doubtless drive many people in their jobs. But in the long-term, celebrations are stored as positive emotional feelings, while bonus cheques at work are not. They have no meaning; they are simply facts that pass. Celebrations, by contrast, are stored in your memory and recalled anytime we want to give ourselves a lift. And when you achieve a goal and acknowledge it with a celebration, it will make you feel more positive about the challenges ahead. The athletes going for the gold medal or the world record are visualising success in ways that are entirely personal, not in relation to the money they can make from advertising or product endorsement.

> Celebrate something every day, make it a habit

Look along the timeline of your ambitions and the celebration of success, no matter how small, will inspire you. As a result, you will look forward to the future and move towards it confidently. Money may come with success, but it is neither a substitute for, nor a measure of true success: it is a by-product. And at the end of your life you will not remember money, you will not find meaning in it. People who have had life-threatening illnesses or near fatal accidents, have had the fragile nature of life deeply impressed upon them. For them, every day is a celebration, and yet all too often we lose contact with that simple fact – we're alive. It is a great shame that we have forgotten to celebrate even this. We can do it in the simplest and smallest of ways – a smile to a person at a bus stop, a kind word to an elderly person sitting on their own in the park, taking the time to look someone in the eye. Just celebrate being alive. I think it's marvellous when you watch young children playing innocently, full of enthusiasm in a world of possibilities. And when someone in their game scores a goal, they jump up and down for joy, or sometimes they get sad, living life with all it's emotional dramas. They find simple pleasures and enjoy them. How often these days do we take pleasure in simple things?

> Our success is not a measure of what we earn or what we have, it is measured by what we become

I read somewhere that there over a thousand statues in New York City – statues to engineers, pilots, architects, politicians, fireman and policemen – but there is no statue to a critic. Critics criticise, of course; they look for the fault and bring the world's attention to it. I would ask that you focus entirely upon your successes, and celebrate them all along the way. There is no short cut to success in life, no quick fix; it is seven days a week, 24 hours a day; it is a state of mind based on a belief and a conviction, that whatever we believe and dream we can do, we can. And when we achieve it, we will measure it not by what we earn or what we have, but by what we become.

REMEMBER

- Celebrate every success – it reinforces our self-image as that of a winner
- Celebration is not measured by scale – but by sentiment
- Find pleasure in simple things – celebrate life every day

11

THE WINNER
WITHIN

YOU WERE BORN WITH
THE SEEDS OF
GREATNESS, AND BORN
TO WIN THE GAME OF
LIFE. SOME OF US
FORGOT TO LEARN
THE RULES FIRST

Goodness is the only investment
that never fails.

Henry David Thoreau (1817–1862)

Those who do not feel they are taking steps towards
their goals are five times more likely to give up and
three time less likely to feel satisfied with their lives.

Elliott, M., 1999. 'Time, Work and Meaning', PhD Dissertation,
Pacifica Graduate Institute.

THE WINNER WITHIN

We were born with an inbuilt natural ability to succeed. In attempting to make sense of the world and overcome the obstacles along the path, our minds absorb all the information they receive, and store it away for future reference. A child's mind soaks up information like a sponge: research has shown that the first seven years of life are a critical learning period, and that much of how we think of ourselves is shaped around this time and stays with us until we consciously change it.

As children, we unknowingly set ourselves goals and had the confidence to achieve them; for the most part we were a pretty fearless bunch. Have you ever noticed how naturally a very young child will climb a step-ladder in order to follow his father who's up there painting a window, or go up quite boldly to pet a dog in the park? But at the same time, young children are very impressionable. If a child is told by his mother that there is a monster under the bed ready to grab his ankles if he gets up in the night, that child will believe the statement to be true. This creates a barrier in the child's mind. Fear has taken over by becoming a dominant thought. So what we condition children to believe in and what to expect are extremely important.

> Don't limit yourself by low expectation, raise the bar and aim higher than you had believed possible

Is it *really* true that you can achieve any realistic goal you set yourself? Though such a claim may appear to be the stuff of fantasy, or a popular self-help mantra, I know that it isn't. Your success depends upon your *determining to create* success; it depends on the goals you set yourself, the sacrifices you are willing to make, and the real benefits that you see this success bringing you.

Many persons have the wrong idea
of what constitutes true happiness.
It is not attained through self-
gratification, but through fidelity to
a worthy purpose.

Helen Keller (1880–1968)

Certainly we all want the freedom that financial security gives, but
hopefully we understand that money alone does not bring happiness. A psychiatrist friend once observed that poor people go
through life believing that money will make them happy, and this
thought gives them hope; but his wealthy patients have realised that
it doesn't, and frequently feel they have lost all hope.

To develop our winning potential, to maximise our chances of
success, we need to be honest with ourselves and with others, to
have high standards of personal integrity. Are your goals right for
you – morally, ethically and spiritually? If you want to be successful, you cannot live a life at odds with the values you identify as
crucial to that success. The happiness that comes from purely
material success is often shallow, based perhaps on passing indul-
gence and ephemeral pleasure. In contrast, the success that comes
from being truly happy is a wonderful feeling, a permanent lived-in-
the moment experience.

Take away my people but leave my
factory and soon grass will be grow-
ing on the shop floor; however, take
away my factory and leave me my
people, and we will build another
business.

Andrew Carnegie (1835–1919)

The *Natural Born Winners* approach to success is not a quick-fix solution but a structured programme that will help you on the journey from where you are now to where you want to be in the future. And it will do so without compromising your standards – indeed, it may well confirm and consolidate them. Your integrity is a quality you can only lose once – so don't compromise it.

An American high-school coach always called his students, 'Champ.' When asked why, he said it was because he wanted them all to go through life thinking of themselves as champions. To create the future that you want, think of yourself as a champion. Just as you must take responsibility for your physical well-being by following a healthy diet and exercise programme, so to achieve a successful mind-set you have to train your mind. And just as exercise and diet will *condition* your body, it is equally within your grasp to mentally develop a permanent sense of happiness and well-being.

We grow up with many natural talents, but such is our longing for social acceptance within our peer group that, in order to fit in, we hide them. You now can rediscover, develop and use those talents.

MOTIVATION

Much has been written on motivation, but what exactly is it? The word 'motivation' brings to mind *motive* and *action* – when you are seeking to achieve something you *move* towards your objective. But what *is* your motive? Is yours internal or external, or both? Whatever it is, it's the force that will drive you on.

Identify what motivates you; your internal motive will be your determination to change. Internal motivation can be very powerful if it is a deep-felt commitment that comes from your purpose and passion. A group of people decide to give up alcohol for the month of January: the ones who do it successfully once, can do it every year because they are internally committed to doing so. External motivation is equally powerful: little is more likely to stop you drinking than being told by the doctor that your liver will pack up if you don't.

We can motivate ourselves towards an object – a new car, for instance. You could also cut out a picture of the car, stick it on the wall above your desk and every day look at it and visualise owning it. Your determination to own it would be the internal motivator; the picture of the car, the external one.

We don't remember days; we remember moments.

Cesare Pavese (1908–1950)

Our motivators vary according to our goal. Early man was driven by a need for food and shelter, for without food he would have starved and without shelter he would have been exposed to danger and the elements. For the fortunate majority in our society, starvation and exposure are almost non-existent, and so in the modern world we are motivated by other needs: we week financial security, to provide for our families and to guard our personal safety.

WHAT ARE YOUR NEEDS?

I took a mini-cab in London once, driven by a Ghanaian. On his dashboard was a picture of three small children. I asked him if they were his, he said with great pride that they were and that he was hoping they would be able to join him in England soon. I asked him how he enjoyed being a mini-cab driver. It was OK, he said, because he earned money from it; he was, by profession, a qualified engineer but could get no engineering work over here, so he kept the picture of his children there to remind him constantly of why he was driving the cab twelve hours a day, seven days a week.

For the cab driver, this photograph was a powerful reminder of his deep need (to care for, support and be reunited with his family). You too have needs that you have to identify in order to help motivate yourself. Many goal-setting techniques use pictures and other images as motivators, encouraging you to construct a clear vision of the future you want – the house, the car, the holiday or whatever it may be. Consolidating this vision involves continually referring back to the image as well as repeating daily positive affirmations that rein-force the subconscious emotional memory. It is a powerful tool, don't underestimate it.

Setbacks and crises can be great motivators. Many people who lose their jobs later say it was the best thing that ever happened to them. It forced them to focus on what they really wanted to do with the rest of their lives; it motivated them away from their comfort zone. But motivation without a firm and resolved faith in our ability to succeed will never be truly effective. Also, when motivation is purely personal or self-interested, it is generally more difficult to keep it going day by day than when it is employed in the service of others. When the greater good is at issue, then motivation is more powerful because it is supported by values that have purpose.

In business, although people may initially be motivated by money or perhaps by power or position, these do not necessarily remain the most important factors. One American company conducted a survey in which they asked supervisors to rank the importance of ten motivators for their employees. Then they asked the employees to rank the same list in order of what they most wanted from their supervisors.

The results are shown on the following page.

Time and time again companies pay lip-service to the importance of appreciation and involvement, and yet they spend so much energy motivating their staff only through incentive schemes, loyalty pack-ages and money. They're missing the point. Of course money is a motivator, but not the only one. A word of praise is priceless.

A study done in Massachusetts into the causes of heart disease asked participants two questions: 'Are you happy?' and 'Do you love your work?' The results showed that those who answered yes to both were statistically less likely to get heart disease.

Your core values and your passion for what you are doing are the strongest motivators when it comes to how you act, think and work.

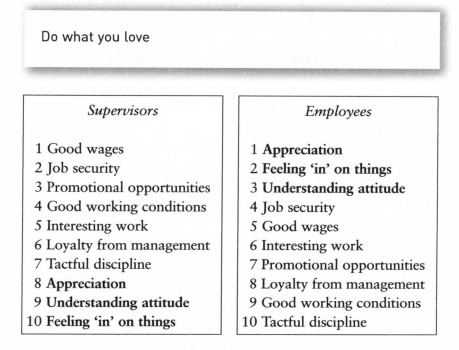

Do what you love

Supervisors	Employees
1 Good wages	1 **Appreciation**
2 Job security	2 **Feeling 'in' on things**
3 Promotional opportunities	3 **Understanding attitude**
4 Good working conditions	4 Job security
5 Interesting work	5 Good wages
6 Loyalty from management	6 Interesting work
7 Tactful discipline	7 Promotional opportunities
8 **Appreciation**	8 Loyalty from management
9 **Understanding attitude**	9 Good working conditions
10 **Feeling 'in' on things**	10 Tactful discipline

What is *your* passion? Identify it and get it to work for you. The pursuit of your personal success won't necessarily bring with it great riches; but it just so happens that when we achieve personal success, we automatically create wealth for ourselves, and wealth comes in many forms.

YOUR CORE VALUES

What are *your* supreme values?

Are you always fair, honest, kind, humble, helpful, trustworthy, courageous? If asked, we would all wish to say, yes, more or less, to most of these questions.

But if your values are at odds with your goal, success will almost certainly elude you – or if it doesn't elude you, it won't last long because it will be built on shallow foundations.

Let me ask you a question. To achieve your goal would you steal?

Would you make a false claim? Would you lie? I hope you said an immediate no! Yet we have all at some time told white lies so as to spare people's feelings, or rewritten our CVs to fiction-prize winning standards. And we've done it and fully justified it because we've believed the end justifies the means. But we've also known, at heart, that no amount of justification could make it right, and that we are only fooling ourselves.

Strive to create for yourself an ethical standard of which you can be proud and that others will hold up as an example of personal excellence. As the saying goes, 'If you are suffering from lack of self-worth, perhaps you are not doing anything worthwhile.'

I am not talking about being a goody-goody, a saintly figure far removed from the common run, but I *am* talking about personal integrity. In the pursuit of personal and professional success it *is* important that you do the right thing. That you *don't* cheat, steal or lie, even in ways that may be regarded as socially acceptable or even justifiable. There are few of us who haven't at one time or other said things like, 'Well, everyone does it,' or 'Someone did the same thing to me.' But once you corrupt your ethical standards in such ways, even just a little bit, a rot quickly set in.

Racquetball player Ruben Gonzales got through to the final in his first professional tournament and had to play the defending champion. In the last moment of the match he hit a shot down the line that was called 'in' by both judge and line judge. He had won his first pro-tournament, it seemed. But Gonzales lost no time in telling them that the shot had actually gone out and they'd misread it, and he asked for it to be played again. It was, and he lost the tournament. He was asked later why, at such an auspicious moment, he had challenged the judges' decision and allowed his opponent back in. He answered simply that it was because he knew the ball was out, and he could not have allowed himself to claim victory. His integrity was not for sale.

Think about what your core values are. Identify them and strive to live them every day.

RESPONSIBILITY

We all make mistakes, and we all have a personal responsibility to ourselves, to the people we interact with and to the world at large. How we deal with our mistakes can crucially affect the outcome of our future behaviour. Too many of us blame others for our mistakes. No matter how we look at it, when things go wrong we all have a personal responsibility for which no one else is accountable. We may say, 'The reason I'm like I am is because when I was a child I didn't get any love,' or 'It's not my fault I'm late – I've always been late' – acknowledging the problem but accepting no responsibility. But we must accept in the end that we are the person we *choose* to be.

Remember that the one thing in your life that you have total control over is your attitude. We've seen that you can learn new perspectives that will improve it. It's not easy, changing a lifetime's habits – but rest assured that if you can imagine it, you can do it. Also accept your failures along the way. I have said many times how vital it is that you learn not to identify yourself with failure but to see it as a learning experience.

Live your own life. Don't waste time comparing yourself with others – you may be unaware of how little you know about their situations or their aims in life. When I was at the Royal Marsden Hospital, I was told never to discuss my case with anyone else because they might well offer me information or opinions that bore no relationship to my case, but that might nonetheless affect my feelings about my illness in unhelpful ways. Don't judge others, either. You may know next to nothing of their situation and circumstances.

Don't compare yourself to others – it leads to envy or to arrogance; two characteristics you are better off without

Your life is your responsibility so take control, get in the driving seat and follow your heart towards your distant star. For many people this feels impossible because feelings of inadequacy, of unworthiness and self-loathing, or a history of persistent failure sits like an unwelcome visitor on their shoulder and whispers in their ear 'You'll never do it. You can't succeed. Buying self-help books won't make any difference – you're a loser.'

Try as you might this voice cannot be shifted – or can it? I have a very simple exercise I give to help others with this problem: very simple, but very effective. Sit quietly and reflect on those doubts then, simply and with feeling, forgive yourself for this sense of inner shame. That's it. Oh – one more thing as you do it. Add 'I am a good person, I will succeed' and whenever negative thoughts or feelings creep in, repeat, 'I am a good person. I will succeed.' You will immediately have begun rebuilding your self-esteem, and all because you have taken responsibility for your feelings, stopped identifying with them and begun to move on.

PERCEPTION

We have all witnessed 'magic', whether on the stage or on television. A certain trick leaves us amazed at what has happened – we've just witnessed something that's impossible! Of course, it was all to do with what we *saw*, as opposed to what was actually happening. Quite simply, we were the subject of misdirection or illusion.

> We don't see things as they are. We see them as we are.
>
> *Anaïs Nin* (1903–1977)

What you see, hear and believe dictates how you respond and act. Life experience and personal belief all shape your perceptions of the world, yourself and your future. If you want to change the way you see the world and act in it, you must let go of your negative perceptions and beliefs and create a new and honest vision of your future. When someone says, 'I wish I could change my nose, because the one I've got is too big,' they believe without any doubt that it's their nose that's holding them back. This conviction affects the way they feel about themselves and becomes the reason for much unhappiness and lack of fulfilment.

Examine the way you think, examine your most deeply held beliefs. Ask yourself whether these perceptions are truthful and honest or no more than illusions that you have created.

JOY

The pursuit of happiness without a purpose is impossible, because the mind needs to identify clearly with a goal. Given that our happiness is not going to reside solely in the acquisition of material goods, power, rank or position, we must find a purpose that transcends these things.

Joy is not in things, it is in us.

Richard Wagner (1813–1883)

I'm not suggesting that this necessarily involves some complex spiritual or philosophical quest. True winners are those who realise their true potential, and they do so by consciously having found goals with purpose and meaning. We witness the opposite end of the spectrum in people who pursue temporary oblivion through drink or drugs in order to bring brief relief to lives that have *no* meaning or purpose.

Many years ago a friend from Glasgow told me of a long period when he had been in the depths of depression. Questions to do with the purpose and meaning of life haunted him, and he could find no answers that gave him any comfort. Though he'd been brought up a Christian, he was not religious; he had seen too much religious hypocrisy, and had chosen not to have any beliefs. Having been driven to near-desperation by his feelings of helplessness and hopelessness, unable to sleep, he got up very early and drove aimlessly, eventually ending up in a car park near Loch Lomond, a beautiful spot 25 miles from Glasgow. He sat in the car and in an moment of understanding, realised that his purpose in life was simply to do his best, to leave the world a better place than he had found it and to help as many people along the way as he safely could. It seemed at the time too cute a solution to me, too simple, but since it was clearly helping him I questioned it no further. I have come to realise it as truth.

I didn't recognise it until much later, but the fact was that he had indeed found his sense of purpose. He had discovered the very core values that brought everything else into perspective. For him these values involved doing his best in the service of others, and their discovery released him from his painful anxiety, his sense of worthlessness, his paralysing lack of direction. I believe our lives are journeys of self-discovery. Ultimately the values and true success that we seek are realised at a spiritual level when we reach the understanding that success, joy and happiness lie not in things, places or people, but within ourselves. Nevertheless, sometimes being nice for the sake of it has its own rewards, whatever you believe.

When you are ninety-six years old and your parachute fails on your first sky-dive somewhere over the Nevada Desert, your life will flash in front of you and I will make you a promise: you will not remember your gold watch, your fancy car, your top-of-the-range clothes or your property portfolio. I also very much doubt that the memory of reading this book is going to flash through your mind either. What I do know is that you'll remember those moments in your life when you were fully involved, fully belonging and fully appreciated: those moments when you gave yourself completely to whatever it was you were doing and whoever you were doing it with or for. The birth of your child, the smile of a loved one, the jumping for joy when your team won a match: you will see those times for what they were – times when you were fully alive. Celebrating and experiencing joy. Being loved and loving unconditionally. Living in the moment of glory.

You will find, as you look back upon life, that the moments that stand out are the moments when you have done things for others.

Henry Drummond (1851–1897)

APPRECIATION

Do you appreciate yourself? Do you often tell yourself, 'Well done!'? Or are you always finding fault with yourself? People who fail to realise their goals, or who have a history of failure, don't recognise or appreciate their own abilities; they are forever finding fault and looking for reasons why they cannot succeed.

So it is important every time you accomplish even a small step towards your goal, that you praise your effort, recognise the moment as a moment. Winners may often be modest and unassuming, but they have confidence in themselves. When a training or study period session is finished they tell themselves very clearly, 'That was good!' And what they are doing is to create a powerful memory of each small achievement.

Appreciation is a great motivator – as you'll know, when you don't get it. Little is more demoralising than our best efforts going unappreciated.

Three magical words – 'please' and 'thank you'. Use them frequently and see what happens

And of course, the opposite is equally true. I remember being on a bus once, and as one of the passengers came to get off he turned to the driver and said, 'Thanks for the ride.'

The driver momentarily seemed taken aback, but then he smiled and said, 'Hey, it's my job, but thanks.' The passenger had simply developed a habit of thanking people who helped him or came into his life in some other way. Think of the times when you've been driving and you've pulled over to the side of the road to let another vehicle through a narrow stretch, and as he passes the other driver doesn't wave, or toot the horn, or smile – he just passes on. How do you feel about that? I always think they could at least have acknowledged me, recognised my existence. On the other hand, when someone does say thanks, the pulling over never seems such an inconvenience, and you feel a little surge of pleasure.

It is one of the most beautiful compensations of life that no man can sincerely try to help another without helping himself.

Ralph Waldo Emerson (1803–1882)

When you praise somebody, when you show appreciation of their efforts – even in very small ways such as by expressing gratitude or showing courtesy – you both benefit. They appreciate your thanks, and you feel good about acknowledging someone's value. But important as it is to appreciate others, above all don't forget yourself. It is by acknowledging your own little successes along the way that your confidence will grow. And as your confidence grows, so your successes will multiply – a powerful, positive and self-fulfilling process will be set in motion.

Many people, for many different reasons, have low self-esteem. They believe they are unlovable, unworthy. Feelings of low self-worth will handicap your ability to develop and you have to find strategies to overcome them. One way to start is by writing out a list of the things in your life that you are grateful for. This will help you to focus on the good in your life, no matter how trivial the things on your list may seem. They will help you to identify with the positive; they will help you to see yourself as a person capable of achievement and enjoyment. Your list may start with just one thing or several: 'I appreciate the sunshine, I appreciate my friends, I appreciate my love of books, I appreciate having a regular income . . .'

Make your list as short or as long as you like, and return to it and add to it whenever you wish. You will have started to create feelings of gratitude, which will gradually transform into feelings of hopefulness and self-worth.

WHAT WOULD YOU DO DIFFERENTLY IF YOU HAD A SECOND CHANCE?

Have you ever fantasised about what you would do differently if you were eighteen all over again, but had your current wisdom and experience? I am sure there are so many things we would do differently, with hindsight.

Here is a simple exercise that I do frequently as part of the *Natural Born Winners* programme.

Look at one aspect of your life that you would like to change. It might be starting your own business, it might be moving to the country, it might be eating more healthily, it might be about having a more balanced and loving relationship with your partner. Just stop for a moment and identify one aspect of your life that you would like to change. Sit quietly; think about your current situation; and then visualise yourself ten years hence, having changed not one bit, exactly the same as you are now. See yourself ten years older, and feel your frustration and anger at your lack of progress. Then, while visualising that scene ask yourself, as if you were now ten years into the future, 'If I could go back ten years and have this chance again, what changes would I make, what would I do? Now stop the visualisation, and realise that you are now living in that day – *the day that you have the chance to change the future.*

The changes you want to make to avoid an unhappy future can

be made now, they are completely within your control. Start them now, immediately. Do it differently. Do it now.

If I had my life to live over again, I'd try to make more mistakes next time. I would relax. I'd be sillier than I have been on this trip. I would climb more mountains, swim more rivers and watch more sunsets. I would have more actual troubles and fewer imaginary ones. Oh, I've had my moments, and if I had to do it all over again I'd have more of them. In fact I'd try to have nothing else, just moments, one after another . . . I would pick more flowers.

Nadine Stair (aged eighty-nine)

Time is the one thing we all have an equal share of. It doesn't matter whether you are the Prime Minister of the UK, or the guy selling newspapers on the street corner. We all have 60 seconds to each minute, 60 minutes to each hour. Don't waste this time – once gone, it never comes back! Put a time frame on every task you want to achieve. With a time frame, it's so much easier to meet your deadline. Do we ever forget Christmas Day? No. Because it's a date that has been set for us.

Remember, you will never have today again

One thing is for sure: we can't go back and change the past. But many of us carry its baggage around and use the past to excuse our present condition or to anticipate future failure. But let's be quite clear – though we can't change the past, we *can* let go of it. We can choose to determine our future. And the best place to start is by living in the present, because that's the bit you control.

There was once a handsome young king who, for all his power and fortune, was bothered by two questions that he desperately wanted the answer to: What will be the most important time in my life? And who will be the most important person in my life? So he issued a challenge to the philosophers of the world, saying that whoever successfully answered these two questions for him would share his wealth. They came from all over the country and beyond, but none had a satisfactory answer the made sense. Then somebody told him of a wise man who lived many days' journey away in the mountains. At once, the king set off.

Arriving at the foot of the mountain where the wise man lived, he disguised himself as a peasant. When he reached the wise man's simple hut, he found him sitting cross-legged on the ground, digging.

'I hear you are a wise man and can answer everything,' he said. 'Can you tell me who is going to be the most important person in my life and what will be the most important time?'

'Help me dig some potatoes,' the old man said. 'Take them down to the river and wash them. I'll boil some water and you can share some soup with me.'

Thinking this was a test, the king did as he was asked. He stayed with the old man for several days hoping that his questions would be answered, but no answers were forthcoming.

So now he pulled out his royal seal, identified himself as the king and denounced the old man as a fraud. He spoke of his anger at wasting days of his life with him.

'I answered your questions when we first met,' the old man replied, 'but you didn't understand my answers.'

'What do you mean?' said the king.

'I made you welcome when you arrived,' the old man went on, 'and I shared my home with you. You should know that the past is gone and the future doesn't exist – the most important time in your life is now, and the most important person in your life is the person you are with now, because he is the one with whom you are sharing and experiencing life.'

There are two things to aim at in life: first, to get what you want and, after that, to enjoy it.
Only the wisest of mankind achieve the second.

Logan Pearsall Smith (1865–1946)

LAUGH MORE

After being released from the high-dependency unit at the Royal Marsden Hospital, I was returned to a small four-bed room. Because of some post-operative discomfort I wasn't sleeping very well and couldn't concentrate on books or magazines. At one point I noticed that two of the other patients in the unit were dozing, but the third was watching the TV. So I put on my headset and idly started to watch too. It turned out to be a very funny programme and painful though it was, I couldn't stop myself laughing. Every time I laughed, the stitches in my abdomen tugged and I yelled out – but I just couldn't stop myself laughing. It was a case of a moment's laughter followed by a moment's agony. I looked across at the other man who was watching, and he was laughing as well; both our beds were silently shaking. At that moment I came alive again to the wonderful power of laughter: I started for the first time to truly feel well again on the inside.

Laugh well and laugh often is good advice; and if you can't find anything to laugh about, you may be taking *everything* too seriously – don't. Relax and be open to those moments of spontaneous joy. Laughing enhances our sense of well-being. Take a lesson from the

American who, diagnosed with cancer, booked himself into a hotel, hired a projector and a bunch of his favourite comedy films, and laughed himself back to health.

The most wasted of all days is that during which one has not laughed.

Nicolas Chamfort (1741–1794)

Do try to see the funny side of things. Often, it's only in retrospect that we can see something that seemed deadly serious at the time as actually quite comical. How much better to be able to relax enough to find the humour in the moment. Soldiers, doctors and people who work in the emergency services use black humour so as to diffuse the distress of the tragedies that they regularly encounter. 'I didn't know whether to laugh or cry,' is something we quite often say. If you have a choice of laughing or crying, it's usually better to laugh. Laughter releases endorphins which flood into our brains and make us feel good, giving us a natural high, that helps dislocate us from all our concerns. Our ability to laugh is a gift from the universe or an evolutionary mistake – either way, make sure you use it.

Cheer yourself up! Do you have any favourite films? I do, and sometimes I'll watch them more than once in the course of a year, maybe just playing a favourite scene. When you smile you automatically increase your feelings of well-being; your mind is triggered by the act of smiling to remember happy memories.

I watched an American comic on a talk show describe a moving conversation he had with his father on his deathbed. The father had been a nightclub comic who had never made the big time, and his son felt that his father's life had been hard and unfulfilled. He recalled his father saying to him, 'You know son, I figure if you go through life making at least one person laugh, every day, you will have made a pretty good account of yourself.' The old comic had made a pretty good account of himself. Given the choice of being deadly serious throughout life or laughing at its absurdities, I know what I would choose – every time.

To laugh often and much, to win the respect of intelligent people and the affection of children; to earn the appreciation of honest critics and endure the betrayal of false friends; to appreciate beauty; to find the best in others; to leave the world a bit better, whether by a healthy child, a garden patch or a redeemed social condition; to know even one life has breathed easier because you have lived. This is to have succeeded.

Ralph Waldo Emerson (1803–1882)

Laughter can be a physical expression of joy and well-being, or just a response to something funny. Look for funny moments in your life, look for things that make you laugh. When you get together with your friends, what stories do you tell each other? Often you find at reunions that you tend to talk about past shared experiences, frequently recalling those moments that made you laugh. And when you laugh, you are taken out of yourself; it's a wonderful feeling.

Never underestimate the power of laughter in your life. Seek it, enjoy it, develop it, be healed by it. Important as it is to laugh at things in life, learn as well to laugh at yourself. Never take yourself too seriously. If you make a silly mistake, laugh at the absurdity of it and move forward. Don't feel embarrassed, anxious or ashamed;

laugh at yourself and learn the lesson. No other species has a sense of humour or the ability to benefit from laughter. Our ability to share in its transforming power did not develop by chance; its purpose may not be clear, but it sure is fun. Make the best of it.

REMEMBER

- Find out what motivates you – use it to fuel your actions
- Your attitude is completely your responsibility – so choose to be positive
- Time is a precious commodity – don't waste your time doing things which take you away from your goal

12

NEW
BEGINNINGS

YOU CAN CHANGE YOUR
LIFE, ANY DAY YOU
WANT TO. IT ONLY
REQUIRES THAT YOU
TAKE POSITIVE ACTION

The greatest discovery of my generation is that a human being can alter his life by altering his attitudes of mind

William James (1842–1910)

Managers of production facilities who are meeting their quality targets actually invest 20 per cent more time in improving their practises, than managers of facilities that are falling short of their goals. In other words, the better off work harder to get even better.

Coulthard, P. 1998. 'The Quality Achieving Behaviour of Work Group Managers', PhD Dissertation, Portland State University.

NEW BEGINNINGS

This chapter will show you how to create and implement a personal blueprint, a life-planner that you can use to achieve both professional and personal success. A word of warning though: remember that it is you alone who have to do it. So all the personal-development and self-help books, all the inspirational audio- and videotapes in the world, all the motivational seminars you may attend and all the encouraging words from friends – none of this will count for a jot if *you* do not commit to making it happen.

If you do what you've always done you'll get what you've always got. It follows that if you are not successful, if your life is not where you want it to be, then it's an absolute certainty that nothing is going to change until you determine to *make* it change – it's that simple

That's the bad news. The good news is that you have the capacity to change your life any day you want to. Don't think of yourself as an old dog that can't learn new tricks. Don't think of yourself as someone so embedded in old patterns that it would be impossible for you to transform yourself. It's never too late to make a change in your life. It really doesn't matter what age you are. So forget that excuse, for a start.

You want to be a success; you really want to achieve your personal goals – OK let's do it.

> When you believe you can, you will begin to see opportunities all around you

So, before you set out to change the world, learn first to change yourself. Change is a difficult thing to achieve. It's no coincidence that we talk of habits being 'broken,' because breaking a habit is often a painful process, and we naturally tend to resist pain. All the same, hard though it may be, habits *can* be broken; and it's when you successfully break one that's been hampering you that you start to believe in success.

Resolve to persist until your goal is realised. It's said, and I know from experience, that in a marathon the last mile is the longest. You never get to find that out until you have run the first 25 and a half, of course. But the point is that you are capable of achieving so much more than you currently believe. In order to make this programme work for you, you must get away from a self-image that restricts your personal growth. See yourself as the success you were born equipped to become. Understand that all change begins with a change in attitude and a change in thinking. Whatever your personal history, you can, if you determine to, break through those inhibiting beliefs.

Whatever you can visualise powerfully and believe in absolutely, you can achieve, and that is a fact not an opinion. It takes proper planning, persistence and unwavering confidence. But once you have all of these you will reach your goal.

'Today is the first day of the rest of your life.' Cliché though this may be, it is nonetheless true. You might equally say that yesterday was the last day of your old life. What has gone before has shaped the person you are. If you don't like that person, determine today that you are going to change. Don't think about what might go wrong. If you need more encouragement, consider these examples. In its first year of business Coca-Cola sold only 400 bottles. Mr Gillette, the man who created disposable razor blades, was at first ridiculed by many companies who said his project was doomed to failure; in his first year of business he sold just 57 of his blades. David Hartman, a young American who went blind at the age of eight, became at twenty-seven the first blind person to complete medical school. Beethoven was totally deaf when he wrote his famous *Ninth Symphony*. The inventor of the 'Post-it' note persisted with his idea even after the marketing campaign had been deemed a total failure and his investors had lost confidence in the product. There are millions of similar examples.

'Success follows your last failure,' so the saying goes; and none of these people knew when their last failure was going to be, but they persevered. Every success has its price; to some it comes easily, for others it takes a great deal of effort. But the common factors are complete belief, dedication and persistence. So with that thought at the front of your mind let's go on now to consider the creation and development of your future success. And if you really want it, you'll do it.

YOU CO.

There is a professor at a university in America who says to all of his new students on their first day, 'If I could buy you for what you think you are worth and sell you for what I *know* you are worth, I'd be a millionaire.'

Too many people undervalue themselves. They have a low opinion of their abilities and of their potential. But if you don't value yourself, who will? In the business world, companies that attract investors are valued for their potential, not simply for their basic financial assets. Equally, you should value yourself on your potential. Think of yourself in terms of what you could achieve, not in terms of what you've done already. You'll be amazed.

Think of yourself as a business, as a good investment for the future! Let's call this business *You Co.* Is it a progressive business or is it risk-averse? What are its resources and morale like? How is it going to grow one day to become *You International Plc?*

In large companies there are diverse departments with different functions – research, marketing, sales, distribution, manufacturing, finance, human resources and so on. They are all working towards the success of the organisation of which they are part. They are meant to complement each other, to work in harmony; if they don't there will be problems. They may operate independently of each other, but if they are not focussed on the same goal, difficulties, will arise.

Just as organisations are made up of departments, so are you: you have distinct aspects of yourself that go into making you the person you are, and it's important that, just like the departments in a company, these should be working in harmony. No individual is greater than his department; no department is greater than the company. Similarly, no one aspect of your life is more important than the others. There is a saying in sport that a champion team can beat a team of champions any time.

To be truly happy and successful you need to be operating as efficiently as a well-run business. So let's substitute the roles of departments and replace them with the individual aspects of your life which need to be performing at their peak. I have identified seven: *self, health, attitude, relationships, spirit, career* and *wealth*. We shall look at these in more detail shortly, but first let's have a status report on *You Co*. How is it doing?

What's your answer? It is just 'OK'? Well, if so, I don't think that's good enough. You deserve to be functioning better than OK. You weren't born to be just 'OK' – you were born to be great.

What does your current life chart look like?

If *You Co*. is doing merely OK, then I don't think I want to invest in it. I want your company to be doing great. I want to back a winner. If your life chart indicates that the main aspects of your life are just OK or worse, then you need to get your life plan on track and operating at a level that will guarantee success.

YOUR SEVEN ASPECTS

When I began creating personal development programmes, I identified seven aspects of my own life that I believed needed to be working at a level beyond OK if I was to stay on track. You may identify in your own life aspects that are important to you but that I have not listed here. Feel free to include them in your life chart. But I do believe these seven are essential, and I would advise you not to neglect any of them.

The bottom axis of your chart contains your seven aspects, and the left-hand axis has the scale. Look at that scale for a moment. At the mid-point I've written 'OK'; below it, 'Could be worse'; below that, 'Sucks'; and at the very bottom, 'Don't ask'. Above 'OK' I've written 'Good'; above that, 'Great'; above that, 'Fantastic'; and at the top of the scale, 'Sensational'. A pretty subjective scale, you may say. So it is. And I suggest you make yours equally subjective – not just one to ten, which is far too precise. Feel free to create your own, one that reflects the way you see things. If 'Fantastic' is your top line, I want you to be operating at Fantastic for the rest of your life. It's what you should be aiming for – and what you deserve!

Let's look now at those seven aspects.

Self

How do you feel about yourself? How do you feel about your future? Do you feel confident that you can meet any challenge face on? How is your self-image – are you comfortable with it? Do you like it? Do you *like* who you are? Are you proud of yourself? Are there aspects of your behaviour that you're ashamed of? How do you look? When you look in the mirror in the morning, do you like what you see?

> After a celebration that had gone on rather late, I woke up the next morning and caught a reflection of myself in the mirror. I did a double take, looked again, then said quietly, 'Dad!' It had finally dawned on me that I was getting older, that I was no longer the fresh-faced youth I imagined myself to be. For a time I felt a bit gloomy about it, but in due course I realised it was nothing to be worried about. It was just part of the process of life.

How do you feel about ageing? Are you ageing well, or is it

something you are not comfortable with? Do you like your own company? How near are you to 'Fantastic'?

Health

By health I mean both your physical and your mental well-being. Are you taking care of yourself? Are you surprised at the way some people treat their bodies? The way they use food and drink and other substances without thinking of the consequences. And their ability to neglect the idea of exercise altogether!

I love watching people on a Sunday washing their cars, checking the oil and the battery, making sure that everything is working just right. They do all this because they can put a value on the car, it's worth a fixed sum of money – they really love that car. But it sometimes seems as if they don't value half as much that wonderfully sophisticated and complex piece of organic engineering, the like of which it is so far beyond our ability to replicate – the human body.

Are you looking after *your* body? And if not, why not? Your health should be a priority. Physically fit people cope with stress much better than the unfit. Make an appointment with your GP for a medical examination, then put together a well-being programme to get yourself fit.

Pay attention to your diet. 'You are what you eat,' the saying goes. There is a great deal of information available on nutrition in bookshops and libraries: which foods to combine with which, what constitutes a good diet, whether generally or specifically – high-protein, low-fat, and so on. Bear in mind in particular that our bodies are perfectly adapted to the foodstuffs available in nature, and try to eat more organic foods. I enjoy the occasional hamburger and fries as much as the next person – but all things in moderation! Don't abuse your body by filling it with junk.

Are you taking *any* exercise? Even the smallest amount will impact positively on your life. Studies of seventy-year-old men who started doing simple weight training showed a decrease in blood pressure and an increase in muscle tone. You are never too old to exercise. Even if for you it means merely walking for five minutes longer or taking the stairs instead of the elevator, still do it.

A very important part of your health is relaxation – stress management. Everyone feels stressed from time to time: the key is knowing how to manage it. We need to learn to relax in a natural, healthy way that is not dependent on cigarettes, alcohol or other substances.

How much time do you set aside for physical relaxation? I meditate in the morning and in the evening. Sometimes I do it only for five minutes, sometimes for twenty, but the benefit to my life is immeasurable. Though I still experience stress, I don't suffer its effects anything like as much as I used to. Yes, there are times when everything seems to be happening at once, but I am able to stay calm even though my mind may be racing. My body doesn't follow suit because I have learned to keep it relaxed. I will share my method with you later in the chapter.

Attitude

Is your attitude positive or is it negative? Are you an optimist or a pessimist? Do you expect the worst and hope for the best?

Your attitude is the one thing you can change immediately. Of course, you won't instantly shed your old patterns of thinking and behaving, but you'll discover that by controlling your attitude, you can genuinely affect the way you respond to situations. Determine that it will be a positive attitude, that you won't let yourself be frustrated or angered by things that got to you before. Your attitude determines not only how you see the world, but ultimately how the world sees you. Get your attitude right, and everything else will become easier. You are looking not for 'OK' – you're striving for 'Fantastic!'

Relationships

I'm talking about relationships in the sense of everyone you interact with – your family and loved ones, your work colleagues, friends, associates – even strangers you come into contact with in the course of a day and may never see again. Whoever you meet you have a relationship with.

How do you relate to them and how do you react to there behaviour? I love this old aphorism: 'Always judge a person by the way they treat another person who can be of no use to them.'

What is your relationship within a team? How do you perceive the team, the people within it and yourself? Do you feel good about it? Do you allow relationships to develop? Or do you close the door and keep people at arm's length? I don't mean you should go round hugging everyone and telling them how wonderful they are. I'm asking you to look at what happens when you meet other people. We all form first impressions, but sometimes we get it wrong and stick to those first impressions too rigidly.

Relationships often show patterns of behaviour. What are yours?

How are you in your close relationships? Do you have a pattern of difficult relationships with your boss? Do your relationships with authority show a pattern of conflict? Do you have a pattern of dysfunctional intimate relationships?

Are you putting in the time to maintain loving family relationships? Do you spend time with members of your family, supporting them and being supported by them, or is work taking up all your time? Are you too busy trying to make it today to worry about your family tomorrow? Does your work take priority over your family? If you have one, your family is your bedrock. If you haven't any immediate close family, close friends can become the support system that a family would otherwise provide. To have a 'family' that unconditionally accepts us is important in all our lives.

I said earlier that at the end of our lives we remember the times when we were most involved and appreciated. There is nowhere else that you are more involved or more appreciated than within your family, whatever form it may take. For some, a religious -

community, a military or other organisation, becomes their bedrock – and provides them with a support that they enjoy for the rest of their lives.

How is your relationship with your family?

Spirit

You have a spirit that is timeless and eternal. It is the essence of your being; it is and always has been part of the universe. I hope that makes sense, and doesn't sound like fluffy esoteric nonsense. I think of the spirit as the capacity to love; if you are not comfortable with that, think of it simply as personal energy that exists though you may not be aware of it. And the spirit connects us to the world seen and unseen – for example, the love you feel for your close family is as much a spiritual connection as an emotional connection. It transcends emotional feelings, it is a pure love that is timeless and unchanging.

Our sense of spirit helps us realise our true self and enables us to find our true purpose, which is doing what we love. For those who have a spiritual or religious belief, they know it as their soul. But no matter what you believe, there is a spiritual dimension to who you are.

Do you have good intentions? Are you honest, sincere, genuine? If you follow a spiritual path, do you do spiritual exercises, pray, go to religious services? Do you meditate and reflect upon what it is, in fact, that you are doing with your life? Do you know right from wrong? Do you help others unconditionally? Do you give of your time or money to helping those less fortunate? Such questions as these will allow you to discover where you are spiritually. So it doesn't matter if you are a committed Christian, Muslim, Buddhist or atheist: we all have a spiritual quality to our being. You need to connect with it, for a keen sense of spirit puts into meaningful perspective so many other aspects of our lives. I went on a spiritual journey of exploration and discovered my soul. In the same way our physical bodies respond to exercise so too does our spirit. And as the Beatles sang 'All you need is love . . . love is all you need.'

Career

It's important not to feel defined by the job you do, but a big part of our lives is determined by how we earn our living – our career. Have you chosen the career you wanted, or has it been chosen for you by circumstances over which you felt you had no control?

Do you have a clear goal? Does it fit in with the future that you see for yourself? Are there any unresolved issues in your current career that are causing you conflict? Are you motivated by wealth or by happiness? Is the career that you're in really the one for you?

If your career is just OK, then it may be time to think about changing it.

Finally . . .

Wealth

Have you thought about what wealth actually means to you? Do you know what would make you consider yourself wealthy? For some, it's having the unconditional love of family and friends throughout their lives. For others it's a precise sum of money. But I know from my personal experience *that if you take care of the first six aspects in this list, the wealth will take care of itself.*

So take care of your self, your health, your attitude, your relationships, your spirit, and your career – and the wealth will follow.

These are the seven aspects that you need to consider when creating your successful blueprint for the future. Add any others that for you are important. Fill in that life chart, see where you are now, and then determine what you want the chart to look like in the future.

YOU THE BOOK

You've set up *You Co.* Now you have to decide what business it is that you are in. What does *You Co.* stand for? What is it going to do? What are your goals for both its short- and its long-term future?

To do this you will need to write your goals and plans down in a notebook, which we'll call your life book – which is what it effectively is. You'll be able to refer back and add to the goals and plans as necessary, and they will represent your goal journey, your personal blueprint for success. This part of the procedure is similar to what I asked you to do earlier but now we're getting down to the details. And there is no better way to reinforce your goal at a subconscious level than by writing it down. It is very important that you don't shortcut this step.

All businesses start with a plan. They identify what it is they are going to do and how they are going to do it; they project income and expenditure quarterly and annually. There is no one model, of course, no one blueprint for a business plan that fits all. It's the same with your personal plan. The one you create will be the one that works best for you. It will be designed by you and understood best by you. You may wish to make your life book very chart-oriented, or you may prefer simple diary entries. It doesn't matter which – choose what best suits you.

The main thing is that this book is *yours*. The form it takes is up to you. I'll now outline the key steps that I have found to be helpful in the construction of my life book.

Choose a fresh page and write down your list of goals. Don't worry how long the list becomes or how fanciful the goals are. The important thing is to let your brain think freely about the life goals that you want to achieve. Then look down the list and divide them into two categories: realistic goals – the ones you truly believe you can achieve and unrealistic goals – those that you feel (or know) are beyond your physical or mental ability, or just plain impossible. For example, if you're fifty-five it's unrealistic to aim to win an Olympic Gold for sprinting; if you're sixteen, your aim to become a heart surgeon before you're twenty isn't likely to be realised.

Now take your list of realistic goals, and divide them into three categories: short-term (up to one month), medium-term (up to one year) and long-term (one year and beyond). Then, taking a separate page for each, define those goals. You can have two goals or twenty running concurrently – it's up to you.

Once you have written out each page, add on each the date by which you would ideally like to achieve the goal. Now begin working backwards from this date so as to determine the stages you will need to go through. For example, if your medium-term goal is to reduce your blood pressure naturally and reduce your dependency on prescription drugs, and you would like to do this within six months, what stages will you need to go through?

First, you need to research methods of reducing blood pressure through healthy eating and exercise regimes. Find out whether there is a clinic or support organisation in your area that could help and encourage you. Decide what changes in diet you will have to make, then before you begin, speak to your doctor and tell her of your intention to gradually reduce your medication so that you plan in six months' time to be controlling your blood pressure naturally. You will find, more often than not, that you will be encouraged and assisted by others in achieving your goal.

On the same sheet of paper, identify what you believe will be the problems encountered in working towards your goal. For instance, do you have a habit of giving up on things? If so, determine not to give up on this goal. Take it day by day. Perhaps you feel that you don't know enough about your new diet to confidently start on it – again, find the information you need, speak to someone who can give you some tips. Identify your problems, and don't move on until you have found a solution.

Finally, think of a picture or image or catchphrase that you can identify with the achievement of your goal. It could be a photograph of a healthier you mounted on a sheet of paper with, beneath it the words, 'Low blood pressure – the new me!' It could be a written affirmation such as, 'I am getting healthier every day in my pursuit of naturally low blood pressure.' It could be a mantra that you repeat to yourself, 'I feel great on this low blood pressure diet!'

Keep returning to this page. You can change the plan, you can change the stages, and you can even change the completion date. But returning to this page will help you to focus your mind on exactly what it is you are trying to achieve. In summary: identify the goal, write your plan for achieving it, identify the problems and solutions, then see yourself achieving your goal through visual pictures or personal affirmations or both.

YOU THE MOVIE

One of the things that are fundamental to the mind-set of Natural Born Winners is that they can see success before they start the journey. They can clearly visualise their goals. Before your mind can start working subconsciously to help you realise yours, you must be able to visualise them just as clearly.

I would now like to share with you the *Natural Born Winner* method for effective relaxation and goal-planning through visualisation.

Before you can visualise, you must be completely and thoroughly relaxed. Make the time every morning and every evening to do this. If you need to get up early, then do so. Find a quiet room and a chair that is not too comfortable – we don't want you falling asleep! Sit upright in the chair, put your hands in your lap and breathe in through your nose very deeply for a count of five; then exhale through your mouth, slowly and gently, for a count of five. Do this eight to ten times – not too vigorously or you may get a little dizzy at first – and as you do so, say to yourself, 'I am breathing in calm, I am breathing out anger. I am breathing in energy, I am breathing out fatigue. I am breathing in relaxation, I am breathing out stress.' Make every breath a calming and soothing message to yourself. After a minute or so begin repeating slowly in your mind, 'I am relaxing, I am calm.' Let your inner-voice become fainter and fainter until it fades away completely. Pay no attention to any thoughts that come into your mind; let them go. Eventually your brain, unused to such conscious inaction, after initially seeking to distract you will become calm. At first this will be difficult to get used to, but persevere – it will happen.

The purpose of all relaxation and meditation techniques is to relax the body and still the mind. Breathing in and out in a rhythmical manner will help you to relax your body and clear your mind. Like anything worthwhile it takes practice, but the important thing is that you begin.

After about three or four minutes, when you are feeling completely calm, receptive and relaxed, I would like you to visualise your favourite place in the world. Think of a place you love: it might be a beach in the tropics, a street in your home town, a magical place from your childhood fantasies – whatever for you fits the description, 'My favourite place in the world'.

Wherever this place is, see it in your mind's eye. If you can't see it clearly, just think about it and imagine the smells, sounds and feelings you associate with it. You associate joyful feelings with this place. Look around, recognise the familiar sights and experience the feelings of happiness and relaxation that go with it. What do you see? What do you smell? Is there a friend there smiling at you? Feel the comfort and security this place gives you. Feel the joyfulness, the contentment, the emotion of being there.

Now – and even if you're on a beach – I want you to imagine a pair of double doors – these form the entrance to your own private cinema. Design an entrance that you will enjoy looking at, because this will be the entrance you will 'see' every time you practise your visualisation. Now go through the double doors and walk into the foyer. Look around the foyer, and sense that you are somewhere familiar and safe. You will be in the foyer for only a short time, but feel free to let it contain anything you want – for instance, a fireplace with a roaring fire in it, or an armchair, or photographs of yourself or of your loved ones, or of friends past and present. The important thing is that you visualise a scene with strong personal connections, one that activates emotional memories.

Your passage through the foyer prepares your mind with the most positive images of relaxation and security. Next, you are going to enter your own private cinema to make and direct your own movie. So now walk through the foyer, towards another pair of double doors – which mysteriously and with the magic of the movies swing open in front of you. Walk down the central aisle of your cinema and pick a wonderfully comfortable seat wherever you want.

Now the lights dim, the curtains part and on the screen appear the words, 'Previous Highlights'. Project onto the screen a montage of the magical moments in your life, moments full of powerful, positive emotional memories that you will love to watch – and accompanied by your favourite music, if you like.

These memories will trigger in your mind the emotions of past successes. You may see yourself being applauded after making a speech at school; opening the envelope that contained your college acceptance; experiencing your first serious kiss; being told by someone that they love you. You may see yourself scoring a winning goal for the football team that you used to play for, or winning a business account. Whatever images you recall, they will be moments in your life when you felt totally alive. Totally successful. Totally happy.

You are feeling and recognising the emotions that accompany being a winner.

Next, the montage sequence finishes and up on the screen comes, 'Now Showing'. Look at your life as it is! See yourself as you really are, imperfections and all. See yourself sitting bored in the office; see yourself loafing around; see the aspects of your life that you don't like. Now freeze the film, and let those images fade away. Take an image of one of your least favourite habits – yourself biting your nails perhaps – and let it slowly but surely fade away. See in your mind those behaviours, habits and parts of your life that you want to change and mentally see them disappearing from your life. You are now clearly programming your subconscious to alter those images, those things in your life that you don't like and that you really want to stop, or get rid of.

And now the lights seem to dim a little bit more, the curtain goes back further, the screen becomes bigger, the music builds and then onto the screen come the words, 'Future Presentations'. Now you are going to see yourself having achieved your goals. Now you see yourself fit and healthy, sitting behind the desk you have always dreamt of occupying, doing whatever it is that is your goal. And when you have clearly visualised this scene, float out of your seat. It's fine – you're the director, you've got an unlimited budget, you can do anything you want to, so enter into the scene and become a part of it. Feel the clothes you're wearing, become a part of the scene you have created, experience the goal you have always dreamt of and emotionally connect with the feeling that goes with this success.

Make emotional memories of this future event, feel them powerfully, smell the flowers in the garden. Whatever goal you have visualised, become a part of the film you have created, and move from scene to scene as if by pressing a remote-control button. When you have finished return to your seat, watch the curtains close, hear the music stop, see the lights go up. Leave the cinema quickly now, move out of the foyer and back to your beach or wherever your favourite place may be. And then slowly become aware of your present surroundings, slowly breathe in and breathe out, slowly open your eyes and come back to full awareness.

This is the only chance you will have on earth with this exciting adventure called life. So why not plan it and try to live it as richly, as happily, as possible?

Creating such a powerful visual memory helps you to construct the goal that your mind will focus on. Going back to your written plan will further affirm it. In these ways you are powerfully reinforcing your belief in yourself. Subconsciously, the way you think of yourself, the way you act, will be profoundly affected. You will *naturally* take care of your health, your family, your career, and so on, because these things will *automatically and unconsciously* be moving in the direction of your goal.

Some may like to think that this is an irrational or even a mystical process, but in fact it is completely logical. You *can* create new goals and visualise new experiences and, at the same time, find the ability fully to relax. And as you do this more and more often, you will be able to do it more quickly. Don't worry at first if you don't see clear images or hear the sounds you want to hear. With practice, the part of your visual memory that can create your own movies will become fully functional. And you'll be the star.

YOU THE SEQUEL – TO INFINITY AND BEYOND!

Return daily to your visualised future. It will strengthen your focus and help you to decide whether the plan you are following really is working. If it's not, don't change the goal – change the plan. It's natural that you will experience setbacks but, whereas in the past you might have given up or seen these setbacks as confirmation of inevitable failure, now they will vanish into insignificance because you have already had that first sweet taste of success and have started to identify yourself as a winner.

> At the end of our lives we do not regret the things at which we failed; we regret the things we wished for and never attempted.
>
> *Robin Sieger*

Remember, this is *your* life. And your life is as valuable and meaningful as that of anyone who has ever existed on this planet. So determine to live it to the full. Live it in a way that will be an inspiration to others; make it a life that you will look back on with pride.

Today will never come again, so seize it. Don't waste time doing things that do you no good or that distance you from your dreams. Bear in mind that even your relaxation periods – *espe-*

cially your relaxation periods – are time well spent. Though others may think that you are simply sitting there, when you are visualising, you know that it is in those moments that you are visiting your future.

Your life will bring you the joy and success your dream of if only you will embrace it and commit to live it to the full – to live the life you want and to achieve the goals your dream of. I know this: whatever you put into life, life will pay you back with interest

If you can dream it, you can do it.

Walt Disney (1901–1966)

I know that life isn't easy, that the road is long and that it will sometimes transform itself without warning into a treacherous mountain path with hairpin bends. But when you finally get to your destination, it won't be the pain or the hardship or the setbacks that you remember. It will be the satisfaction of having done what you set out to do, with the certain knowledge that a lifetime of future successes awaits you.

Don't hurry. Don't worry. You're only here on a short visit, so don't forget to stop and smell the roses.

Walter Hagen (1892–1969)

Return to this book and to others that have informed and inspired you, there is a wealth of information to be gleaned and so many people who can help you. Don't stand back – ask! I can't make you a winner – you already are one. What I have tried to do is to blow away the smoke of self-doubt and fear that we all experience at some time or another in our lives, and show you the road ahead that is your future, if you want it.

I can wish no more for you than this: that you go on to become the natural winner that you were born to be. And of course, that you enjoy the journey. I know you can do it: and I also know that when you believe you can, and then take action – the magic starts.

REMEMBER

- It all starts with a dream – so dream big and dare to fail
- When you take action – magic happens
- When you believe with all your heart that you can – and take action – you will experience success

EPILOGUE

ROB'S RUN

If you should ever go to the Old Forge pub in Inverie, Scotland you will find a plaque on the wall of the pub, it commemorates Rob's Run. If you have completed the challenge then there is money behind the bar for a pint of Guinness. It's on me. It all began in Bangkok on 25th August 1986, when a beautiful child called Sumitta was born. She was born blind and due to complications at her birth, suffered brain damage. When she was five, her parents, no longer able to cope, gave her to the Pattaya orphanage. The orphanage had been started by chance when, in 1970, an abandoned child was left with Father Brennan, a native of Chicago, who after his ordination in 1960 had gone to work in Thailand. The orphanage is now home to 800 children, with schools for the blind and deaf, a vocational training centre for disabled young adults and a home for street kids.

In 1992 I saw an ad in a newspaper asking for people to sponsor children from the orphanage, so I decided to do my bit for charity and was sent Sumitta's details. I arranged a monthly standing order, and that for a while was that. I felt good about doing something, but I wasn't really doing anything, it was passive charity. In 1996 my fortieth birthday was approaching, and I had decided that to celebrate the occasion I would walk from my friend Tom's remote cottage in Strathconnan in northern Scotland, to the remotest pub on the British mainland, the Old Forge at Inverie on the Knoydart peninsula. The distance was about 73 miles, and I thought it would make a suitably demanding challenge for my advancing years. So I planned and trained for six months, and I also invited a number of friends to join me in what was now simply being referred to as 'the Walk'. Later I decided to use the walk as an opportunity to raise money for Sumitta in Thailand.

I was born and raised in Glasgow, an industrial town with a big heart and a tough reputation, and as a child I always wanted to visit the Highlands and walk through the glens where long ago, I had heard, proud warriors had fought to the last man, in pursuit of their freedom. At the time those glens had seemed another country, so far beyond my reach; but now I stood on the threshold of a journey that I'd dreamt about as a 'wee' boy in Glasgow 30 years before.

The big day came and we set out. The weather was atrocious, with the rain and wind sapping our energy. When, after fourteen hellish hours, two of the party were showing signs of hypothermia (I was one of them), we abandoned the attempt.

The following year I had a second go, but a fellow hiker broke his ankle and again the trip was abandoned. Such money as I had managed to raise for Sumitta stayed in a trust account in the bank, but I still hadn't achieved my goal.

I reluctantly determined to try once more, but this time nobody was available to come with me. To walk alone in such wild terrain is foolhardy and irresponsible, so things were looking bleak. A little disconsolately, I put a map showing the route of the walk on the wall of my office and over the next four months almost everybody who passed through the office saw the map and asked about the trip, but still no takers. Then, two people previously unknown to each other saw the map during visits to my office, asked some questions and immediately volunteered to help.

They each brought excellent skills with them: Steve was a former Australian Army outdoor instructor and Nic an Australian performance coach. I asked Brett, a South African who owned a Land Rover, to help as support driver. They all happened to be working in London, but none of them knew each other. At the last moment I asked my friend Chris Rufford, a doctor and former expedition physician, to join the support team.

The days building up to my third attempt had produced some of the worst weather of the year, especially up in Scotland, and it showed no sign of clearing. One day before our departure I grew increasingly anxious, a pervading sense of the previous failures hung over me. I had attempted the walk twice before – both times the conditions had been brutal, both times I was physically exhausted by the distance and the weather, both times I had failed.

I had begun to believe the walk was an unrealistic goal. Especially now that I had set a personal goal of doing it in under 48 hours.

When we set out on the drive to the start point, it was windy and raining hard. Then quite unbelievably, ten miles from the start, it was as though someone had turned off the tap – the rain stopped, the clouds parted, and the sun began to shine. So at 3.30pm on Friday the 12th June 1998, I began my third attempt at the walk.

Steve and I began the first section and Nic joined us for a night march – a demanding section of the route across a slow and treacherous peat bog. At 1.30 in the morning we reached the second planned *rendez-vous* only to discover that the vehicle carrying the hot food had not got through. We were very disappointed as the hot soup had taken on mythical qualities over the last six miles. I had been going non-stop for ten hours and had covered twenty-six miles. Exhausted, we huddled together on the ground in an attempt to stay warm. After about ten minutes Steve said 'Let's go,' and silently we set off into the darkness for the next *rendez-vous* point fifteen miles away.

Six hours later we met the support vehicle, which had been unable to meet us at the previous *rendez-vous*, as a locked gated had blocked their way. Steve and Nic rested up and promptly fell asleep. I sat down and took a look at my feet for the first time. They were not a pretty sight – four of my toenails had become detached from the nail bed.

After a short rest I set off on the next six mile section with Chris, but my feet were extremely sore and I was exhausted. After 30 painful minutes I told him I was going to quit. The whole project had been too ambitious; I had tried my best, but my feet were a mess, and I was hurting. My support walkers, too, were exhausted. Chris was very supportive of my decision, and after a while we reached the next *rendez-vous* point by a bridge and waited for the support vehicle. Only this time, the difference was when it arrived I would be getting in. We sat there on the bridge, at the foot of the next steep mountain section, contemplating the eight mile stretch that I was no longer willing or able to climb. Apart from the odd passing car, the silence as we sat there was complete. I gazed at my feet and dreamt of a hot bath and a long sleep.

I had by now fully justified my decision to myself, but at the same time I was disappointed. I had given all 100 per cent, but it wasn't enough. I decided that I would have the money for Sumitta released from the trust account and sent to the orphanage and although I had failed, I took comfort from the fact that I'd tried.

Again, the support vehicle didn't arrive. After fifteen minutes of silence Chris gave me a serious look and said, 'You're going over that mountain, aren't you?'

I managed to croak a tired and emotional, 'Yes, I am.'

'Right then,' he said. 'I'd better bandage up those feet of yours.'

I had remembered the words of my friend one day during a training session in Wales, 'You only fail when you quit.'

The vehicle now arrived with Nic and Steve asleep in the back. Chris said he was too tired to make the climb with me, but Brett the driver announced that he would come, even though he was only wearing street shoes. We hiked over the steep section and four hours later, after 22 and a half hours and 35 miles we reached Kinloch Hourn, the overnight resting-place.

The next day, rested, refreshed and with freshly bandaged feet, I walked the final 18 miles with Chris, Nic and Steve. I arrived 46 hours and 22 minutes after leaving the starting-point. I had covered 73 miles. I'd done it. I walked into the Old Forge pub and ordered a pint of Guinness. And then Chris asked me to explain why I had gone on after I had so adamantly decided to give up.

I told him that as we'd walked through the night, Nic and I had discovered that we shared not only a movie we had both enjoyed – *Braveheart* – but also the sentiment of our favourite scene from that movie. The scene is just before the first battle between the Scots and the superior English forces. William Wallace comes upon some Scottish soldiers who are running away. He asks them why. 'Because if we run we'll live, and if we stay we may die,' comes the reply.

To which Wallace replies, 'Fight and you may die, run and you'll live – for a while. And dying in your beds many years from now, would you be willing to trade all the days from this day to that for one chance, just once chance, to come back here and tell our enemies that they may take our lives, but they'll never take our freedom?'

As I'd sat on that bridge exhausted and dejected, I'd thought about the strangers, now my companions, who had seen the map on my office wall and had given their time to support my dream, and I'd thought of the miraculous lift in the weather. But most of all I'd thought of Sumitta: I had promised myself I would actively raise money for her.

I thought then, what would I give, one year from now, to come back and have this chance again? I had been looking for reasons to quit, not reasons to keep going. I remembered that the winner is simply someone who gets up one time more than they fall over. I know we all have the ability to dig a little deeper, persevere a little longer, and in my temporary discomfort I had been seeking to take the easy option. So as long as I could put one leg in front of the other I was not going to quit. To keep going was no longer a hardship, it was a privilege.

The next day, less than one hour after we left Knoydart, it clouded over and the stormy weather which had besieged most of Scotland that weekend, returned. I couldn't help thinking both at the time and since, about the truth of some words written in 1951 by W.H. Murray who was on the critical reconnaissance expedition to Mount Everest with the Scottish Himalayan Expedition. He wrote,

> Until one is committed there is hesitancy, the chance to draw back, always ineffectiveness. Concerning all acts of initiative (and creation), here is one elementary truth, the ignorance of which kills countless ideas and splendid plans: that the moment one definitely commits oneself, then Providence moves too. All sorts of things occur to help one that would never otherwise have occurred. A whole stream of events issues from the decision, raising in one's favour all manner of unforeseen incidents and meetings and material assistance, which no man could have dreamt would come his way.

Appendix:

YOUR BRAIN

YOUR BRAIN IS THE
SEAT OF THOUGHT,
DESIRE, WILL-POWER
AND BELIEF. NATURE
SPENT 240 MILLION
YEARS PERFECTING IT.
USE IT!

It is not enough to have a good mind; the main thing is to use it well

René Descartes (1596–1650)

Total number of synapses in cerebral cortex = 60 trillion (yes, trillion)

Shepherd, G. M., 1998. *The Synaptic Organization of the Brain,* Oxford University Press Inc., USA.

YOUR BRAIN

All achievements, from the grandest to the most humble, began life in one person's imagination as an idea. We think and dream in images, and those dreams and images exist only in our minds, so it's worth taking a look at the old grey matter. Actually, the brain is more of a beige colour, so to be technically correct I suppose we should call it 'the old beige matter'.

Much has been written about the brain, yet it is still the least understood part of the body. Experts tell us that we utilise only 5 per cent of its potential, and that the brain is more powerful than the world's mightiest computer. The most important thing to understand about the brain is that how we think dictates everything we do, and though genetic inheritance may account for 50 per cent of our mental process, that still leaves 50 per cent that we can develop and control.

Consider just how much the brain is capable of. Think of John Milton in his old age memorising *Paradise Lost*, or of Mozart having composed, by the age of thirteen, concertos, sonatas, symphonies, an operetta and an opera. We have all heard of people with extraordinary mental abilities in mathematics and in memory, but the interesting thing is that such abilities don't necessary conform to conventional models of intelligence. Take the condition known as autism, for many years one of medicine's mysteries. People suffering from autism are classified as socially dysfunctional and have serious learning difficulties, yet some of them are capable of the most extraordinary feats of memory, and have outstanding mathematical and musical abilities.

So let's be clear – your brain is not just the most complex organ in your body, it's the single most evolved organ in the world. It is living matter, it has the capacity to regenerate itself, and every memory that it stores it can recall for future use, for the whole of your life. It never switches off; it never stops working; it is the source of all our experience, our hopes, our beliefs, our intuition –

ourselves. And, as the brain is the home of all our thoughts, dreams and ambitions, the better we are able to understand and develop the thinking process, the more rapidly we shall increase our efficiency and progress towards our goals.

When compared with earlier research, advances since the 1960s in explaining the brain's complex neurophysiology have been phenomenal, but the more we discover the more we realise we are still just scratching the surface.

Nonetheless, there are some fundamental insights we can gain into the structure, and function, and the thinking processes of the brain, that will put into perspective the *Natural Born Winner* techniques of mentally conditioning one's approach to success. I've always thought the brain is nature's greatest creation – unfortunately it came without an instruction manual, and the sooner we harness its potential, the better.

ITS STRUCTURE

Detailed analysis of the structure of the brain – unless you are studying to be a neurosurgeon – is rather tedious which is due in no small part to its being this very complex organ full of unpronounceable names. So I shall endeavour to keep this as jargon-free as possible.

As you can see from my excellent diagram, the brain is made of up three parts: the brain stem, the cerebellum and the cerebrum. From the evolutionary perspective, the stem was the first part of the brain to develop – around 270 million years ago, give or take a day or two. The first land animals were reptiles, and the stem, this first rudimentary part, is known as the 'reptilian brain'. It controls the information coming in from our physical senses, as well as undertaking basic housekeeping duties such as breathing and heartbeat. It doesn't do any thinking or feeling, and has no emotional centre – which explains why lizards can eat their own young, and don't make affectionate pets.

Next to evolve – about 40 million years later – was the cerebellum, which looks like a bit of rather old cauliflower and lies

Robin's simple guide to the brain

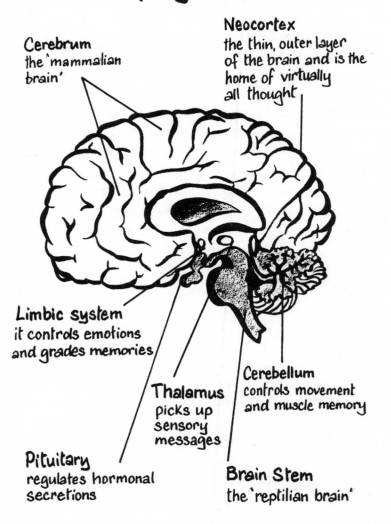

Cerebrum
the 'mammalian brain'

Neocortex
the thin, outer layer of the brain and is the home of virtually all thought

Limbic system
it controls emotions and grades memories

Thalamus
picks up sensory messages

Cerebellum
controls movement and muscle memory

Pituitary
regulates hormonal secretions

Brain Stem
the 'reptilian brain'

behind the brainstem. Its function is to coordinate muscle movements and develop muscle memory, which allows you to walk down the road without any conscious thought for balance or for the movements of your arms and legs. Top athletes work to develop strong muscle memory, so that in the heat of competition they don't have to concentrate on controlling their actions – they just happen naturally. Muscle memory improves throughout childhood, and its early development can be observed when a small child tries to catch a ball. Initially his movements are very un-coordinated, but by repeating the action he allows the process to develop, with some children learning faster and achieving higher skill levels than others. (Which has to be why I dropped that match-winning rugby pass when I was twelve – *must* be.)

The third part – about 160 million years old – is the cerebrum, and this is where, as a student I started getting confused. It is also known as the 'mammalian brain' (which explains why dogs are affectionate and *don't* eat their young), and is the location of our thinking and emotions. The particular features of the cerebrum as it has developed in *Homo sapiens* constitute a vital part of what distinguishes us as human beings, and the rest of this chapter will try to help you avoid its complexity while fully appreciating its extraordinary potential.

In the early days of brain research, scientists thought that the different parts of the cerebrum held different information – one area stored knowledge on geography, for instance, another on friends' birthdays, and so on. It is now accepted, however, that each memory and thought links up different areas of the brain, and this aspect of brain function is called 'multiple mapping'. Multiple mapping is very important, for two reasons:

1 The whole brain is used in the thinking process and in the creation of memory, it is important in its role of keeping the brain's internal lines of communication (the neurotransmitters) healthy and functioning – this is just as important as keeping your arteries unblocked.

2 Memories are stored in different locations within the brain so that it is almost impossible completely to 'destroy' a memory.

Which is good to know. But, of course, the brain doesn't just control thoughts and memories. It is responsible for how we feel, too.

A QUICK GUIDED TOUR OF YOUR EMOTIONAL CENTRE

The limbic system began to evolve about 150 million years ago, and its development marked the creation of social cooperation within animal species. The system is made up of five parts, which collectively act as a kind of switchboard between the mind and the body. As we've already noted, the development of a winning approach to the future, how you think and feel about yourself is initially at least as important as what you do. So bear with me while I run through another bit of the dry subject of brain structure. It will give you an idea of why it is that how we think impacts directly on our self-image and behaviour. And why if we change the way we think we can change our lives.

First stop the hippocampus, the brain's memory centre. This is a temporary repository for short-term memories, and a few longer ones, but it transmits most of our short-term memories out to a location in our neocortex (where, of course, they become long-term memories). The hippocampus operates largely as the place where we hold 'unemotional' facts – learned information such as school subjects with which we have no emotional association. It doesn't fully develop until a person is two years old, and researchers believe that this explains why we have no memories of early infancy. Interestingly, the hippocampus is the first area of damage when an individual develops Alzheimer's, a disease that causes the loss of short-term, but not long-term, memories. (Long-term memories are protected because they are already stored in the neocortex.)

Next, the amygdala, which processes emotional memories. It works with the thinking brain to decide how much emotional impact each memory will carry – your first day at school, your first kiss, the news of a national tragedy. If (and I certainly wouldn't recommend this) you were to have your amygdala surgically removed, you would be totally without emotional response, just like the lizard mentioned earlier. But, of course, this wouldn't bother you because you would be incapable of having any feelings about it.

Closely connected to the amygdala is the hypothalamus which, by relaying any given message to the pituitary gland, triggers the release of hormones, which tell the body how to respond to different situations. For example, when you find yourself in a situation that frightens you, adrenaline is released into your bloodstream, producing the 'fight or flight' response.

Next is the thalamus, part of whose job is to make sense of the constant flow of messages coming in from your sensory organs (with the exception of smell); and finally your pituitary, a pea-sized object that through hormonal control tells the other glands in your hormonal system what to do.

Now, I would be the first to admit that this is a very simplified explanation of brain structure and emotional function, but when we come to apply it to mental conditioning and performance function you will see that it helps to complete the picture. It's important to realise that every experience creates a memory with an emotional association. If, for instance, your emotional memories of failure are strong, when you face a new challenge memories will be recalled with their associated physical feelings. In fact, all future challenges will trigger a similar emotional sensation, so what we need to do is to find techniques for changing this negative pattern of response, and replace it with powerful positive images of future success.

CONSCIOUS THOUGHT

Conscious thought is the state of mental awareness in the here and now. The reading of this book is a conscious act. You are fully aware of it, and you completely control it. Conscious thought is about awareness and choice. It is this ability to weigh up information and make decisions using stored memories and present experience that makes us a unique species.

All the same, the conscious mind for all its extraordinary power, is effectively capable of only one thought at a time, just like a radio can be tuned in to only one station at a time. For example, have you ever had a conversation with someone while simultaneously trying to eavesdrop on another? It's virtually impossible. Or imagine trying to juggle three balls by consciously attempting to control each individual ball. It cannot be done, because your conscious mind cannot process that amount of information simultaneously.

But although, in order to avoid being overwhelmed by a flood of sensory data, we can be aware of only one thought at a time, the conscious mind gives us full control of our actions. In consequence, we have the power consciously to determine how we feel and respond to given situations. Let me give you an example:

You are waiting for a bus when a car drives through a puddle close to where you are standing, spraying water on your shoes. In a physical reflex action, you jump back. Thereafter your response is a conscious one – in other words, you allow yourself to get frustrated, angry, whatever. On the other hand, if you wanted to, you could equally choose to see the soaking as a random act of chance, wish you didn't have wet feet and determine not to let it spoil your day or upset your equanimity. The point is that you consciously choose your response to a given situation, but that choice is often only the result of habit. Your conscious mind can change your habits – if you choose.

Think of your conscious mind as a computer screen: it can only process one image on its display, whilst simultaneously running many programs. Our conscious minds control what we think about and how we think about it.

This ability consciously to control our thought process is an essential ingredient in the creation of success. If you begin to focus on the positive, to put setbacks in perspective and not dwell on failure, you will begin to act in accordance with a healthy and positive self-image. You and you alone have the ability, if you so choose, to change the way you perceive yourself, and your career. Your conscious mind is your greatest asset when it comes to helping you change patterns of behaviour and how you feel about yourself, and will help you to program your subconscious to create future success.

The fact that what you think is what you create, is of critical importance in achieving success. Winners in whatever field do *not* dwell on the negative, or focus on failure; they consciously avoid these pitfalls. Because if you don't control the way you think, the way you think will to control *you*: you will repeat the mistakes and patterns of the past, and perpetuate or even create the very future you wish to escape from. So the first lesson is that it's up to you – and you can do it.

THE SUBCONSCIOUS

Your subconscious collects and collates all the experiences that the senses pick up throughout your life, and stores them for future use. You know those golden Eureka! moments when the solution to a problem, or a brilliant creative insight, just comes to you? Or you suddenly remember an old schoolteacher's name, or pick up a crossword puzzle that stumped you an hour ago only to discover that you can now solve the remaining clues? These are perfect examples of the subconscious doing what it does best. Once your conscious mind had given it the problem, it never stopped working on the crossword puzzle or trying to locate the teacher's name among your long-term memories until it came up with what it was searching for.

Take a simple example of the subconscious at work. Have you ever walked into a store when shopping for a pair of shoes, and found that from the hundreds of pairs on display one suddenly jumps out at you? Why is this? The explanation is that your subconscious scanned all the shoes, compared them with its stored information about your preferences, memories and associations, then, having sent the message to your conscious mind, in a split second, automatically drew your attention to a particular pair.

If you had to explain why your eye initially fell on that particular pair, you might well talk of a 'feeling' that you find hard to articulate. It's certainly not a decision – that's for conscious thought. However, when the assistant starts showing you other, similar, pairs, you may now start consciously overriding the choice you made intuitively. And what you'll certainly find is that any conscious decision you make about the shoes will be much less rapid than the subconscious one. Why? Because unlike the subconscious, the conscious mind can only do one thing at a time.

When we read about the brain's ability to carry out millions of actions simultaneously, we tend to think, 'Impossible!' This is because we are able to be aware of only one thing at a time. Consider how, at a basic level, the brain manages our bodies – usually in ways of which we're quite unconscious. Every function of the body is being regulated all the time; every one of the millions of receptors around the body – to do with heat, pain, pressure, balance, etc. – is constantly passing feedback to the brain, giving it a continuous 24 hour status report. Depending on the information the brain receives, it instructs the body to respond accordingly. For instance, when we get too hot the brain responds by telling the body to begin sweating. Try right now consciously to make yourself sweat – impossible (unless you're a fakir). I know I can't do it. Yet the brain has evolved to do this automatically, along with a million other functions, and is still operating at only 5 per cent of its potential capacity! And, as hypnosis demonstrates, the subconscious can be programmed to reduce your heart-rate, lower your temperature and even anaesthetise parts of your body. These extraordinary abilities, the result of actively conditioning the subconscious, highlight – if only at a physical level – the incredible potential we all have inside us to achieve anything we set our minds to. The creative visualisation technique in Chapter 12 is us actively programming our sub-conscious.

In September 1985 I awoke one morning in a most unusual position, a position I'd never been in before and have never since woken up in. I was lying on my front with my left forearm across the back of my head, the fingers of my left hand resting very lightly on the right-hand side of my neck four inches below my ear. It was not a particularly comfortable position, but before I was aware of any discomfort, I felt under my fingers the presence of a hard pea-sized lump in my neck. Over the next twenty seconds I felt it from different angles and wondered why I had not noticed it before. When I went into the bathroom and looked in the mirror I could see no evidence of it; however, when

I tilted my head to the left a very small lump protruded from below the skin.

I am not, and never have been, a hypochondriac, but I knew that this lump was bad news. In fact, I believed with absolute certainty that it was cancerous, and my first thought was that it was Hodgkin's disease (a cancer of the lymphatic system), as a close friend of mine had died of it three months previously. I went to see my GP, who told me it was a fatty lump called a lipoma. Later I asked three friends – all doctors, including my brother-in-law – to examine the lump: given that I had no other obvious symptoms, they all deduced that it was an old inflamed lymph node of which I had not previously been aware. By this time I did have one symptom – extreme fatigue – and then a blood test revealed a raised ESR (erythrocyte sedimentation rate), which is a non-specific test, but it indicated that there was something amiss. So my sister, who is a theatre sister, arranged for me to see a consultant surgeon at the Christie Hospital in Manchester.

The surgeon examined me, and said that it was impossible to tell what any lump was and that the only way to find out was to remove it. So a week later I went into the hospital and had the lump taken out. I returned to London, where I had to wait five days for the results. On the day before I was due to travel back to Manchester I actually stopped being anxious and felt for the first time that maybe I had just been imagining the whole episode; the blood test result could have a hundred possible causes, the exhaustion could be due to working long hours.

That evening I went to my sister's home for supper – it was her husband who had done the original blood test. Going into the kitchen at one point, I found him on the phone, grim-faced, my sister standing beside him. 'I think he should be told,' I heard him say, and then he saw me. Turning towards me he said, 'The results have come through.'

I remember looking at him and saying, 'They're not good.'

'No,' he replied. 'You've got Hodgkin's.'

Why had I woken up in that position all those weeks ago, and noticed a lump that would have taken six or eight more weeks to become obvious? Why had I continued to seek medical opinions until my family, frustrated at my persistence, decided to get the matter sorted out once and for all? Why did I feel from the first moment that I had Hodgkin's? Surely not because a friend had just died of it. The incidence of Hodgkin's is one in 35,000, so it was clear that the chances of two friends having it were astronomically remote.

I believed then – and I understand now – that my body was fully aware that something was not functioning as it should. I believe my subconscious drew my attention to the illness – it made me listen to the quiet voice within that we call intuition. I was fortunate to have medical friends and family: even then, it was my conviction that had made me persist after the numerous 'don't worries'. I knew I was not naturally a worrier about health matters, so I paid full attention to my intuition or subconscious.

Paying attention to what the subconscious tells us is of enormous importance in every sphere of life – from choosing shoes to overcoming illness. By extension, I understand now that it is our most powerful ally in helping us as individuals to become winners. When I was first exposed to such ideas, I dismissed them as fanciful. I know now, and from direct experience, that they are the key component of successful living.

WHAT A COMPUTER!

Though the human brain is frequently compared with a computer, this undoubtedly oversimplifies the phenomenal sophistication of the brain and exalts the versatility of the computer. It's not just that the brain is capable of vastly more fact storage and memory access, than the world's most powerful computer. What I think is more remarkable is that, as I've already mentioned, we use only 5 per cent of our brain – or, more accurately, we use all of our brain but only to 5 per cent of its capacity. To put it in perspective, the brain has 100 billion neurones capable of making 50 trillion connections (or synapses). Synapses hold thoughts, which become memories, and if we repeatedly use the same thought we create a strong memory. In turn, memories inform thoughts. So, simply put, by recalling positive memories we create positive thoughts.

But that starter supply of a 100 billion neurones, capable of 50 trillion different connections, is just the beginning. In the last fifteen years scientists have discovered that the number of synapses increases twenty-fold by early adulthood, thereby creating over 1000 trillion connections. Nature is nothing if not economical: it doesn't produce surplus to requirements. It's simply given us a practically infinite capacity to learn and create.

I believe that this remarkable instrument that is the brain, properly used, is equipped to deal with virtually any challenge we face in life, with the exception of certain medical conditions. It can handle hundreds of thousands of actions simultaneously, it never stops working, it's the home of your thoughts, it subconsciously controls all your bodily processes, and it's capable of regeneration. Recent research into the ageing process has revealed that brain function does not deteriorate at anything like the rate previously imagined, and nor does old age impair the brain's capacity to learn. However, since the brain is made of flesh and blood, getting the best out of it means looking after it and using it, because the more you stimulate the brain, the more its performance improves. Imagine that you could increase your brain performance by one degree, to 6 per cent of its capacity: it would then be operating 20 per cent more efficiently than the average brain. Now that would be an advantage, if ever there were one!

Your brain determines your sense of well-being, confidence, happiness and satisfaction. All these states reside in that complex organ, where neurotransmitters such as the endorphins maintain and increase these feelings and critically reduce your vulnerability to stress, your exposure to self-doubt. It follows, therefore, that if you can improve your thinking and your ability to use your brain, you will develop a winning outlook and a positive approach to your goals, which, in turn, will help you to achieve success. It's that simple.

But why is this important? It's important because the critical difference between successful individuals and the rest is not in the way they act, but in the way they think.

Programming made easy

We have looked at how the brain stores all experience for future reference. When early man first discovered the secret of making fire, since survival depended on it, this skill was quickly learned. The brain automatically programmed itself to remember how the fire was made, and it's the same with other life skills that we take for granted. For example, think of those times when you got up in the night and had to make your way to a light switch on the opposite wall. In complete darkness you cross the room, and your hand automatically goes almost exactly to where you 'imagined' the light switch to be. The explanation is that, from your previous experiences of putting the light on or off in the room, you have subconsciously remembered the number of steps, the direction of the switch in relation to the bed and even the required angle of your arm.

Similarly, when you drive along a familiar route, it may sometimes feel as if no sooner have you turned the key in the ignition, then you have arrived at your destination – without any awareness at all of having thought about the process of getting there. This is due to the repetitive thought processes operating at the subconscious level – except, of course, when there is some sudden danger. At this point, thanks to the adrenaline response, we instantly override the subconscious process and take full control again. The important thing to realise is that we can create within our subconscious the same kind of patterns that allow us to drive a familiar route automatically and find our way to the light switch in the dark. It's possible to develop and program a habit of positive, success-oriented thought that operates, subconsciously, 24 hours a day. And the means of doing this are not mysterious, but simple, powerful, mental conditioning techniques. If the physical brain represents the hardware of a computer, then the way we think (the lifelong patterns we have created), is the software: that is, it can be recoded. And in changing the way we think we can unlearn those negative habits and patterns that have created the mechanisms that subconsciously cause us to fail in order to reinforce our negative self-image. Because as long as we *think* we'll fail, we will.

Maintenance

So many people take their health for granted. They abuse their bodies through poor diet and lack of exercise, and compound the situation by drinking too much, smoking, and indulging in other forms of substance abuse. But the brain too, is a physical organ, and the way we think can only be as effective as its capacity to function allows. So it is our personal responsibility to look after it.

Up until the 1990s it was believed that the brain, once formed, was unable to produce new cells. It is now accepted that brain cells are continually renewing themselves by increasing their connections to other cells. Since it is through these connections that thought travels, the more connections the brain is able to form the greater its function becomes. The size of the brain is not important in relation to intelligence – it doesn't matter whether you're the proud owner of a big brain or not. What counts is the number of connections between neurones, and the healthier the brain the greater its capacity for the cells to renew themselves and create new connections.

To help maximise your brain function for the rest of your life, look closely at your diet. There is an old saying, 'What's good for the heart is good for the head,' which we should take as our motto in our task of creating maximum brain function. A good blood supply is critical for the brain: at any one time it requires 25 per cent of the blood pumped by the heart. Brain cells, like all other cells, require oxygen and energy. The only source of energy for the brain is blood glucose and as the brain cannot store its own energy it has to rely on a steady flow of energy-rich oxygenated blood to all parts of it. It follows that anything that impedes the efficiency of cerebral circulation has a direct effect on memory and concentration. This isn't a theory. It's a fact.

Low blood sugar, for example, can biochemically prevent the brain from storing new memories. It is known that one of the side effects of stress is an increased demand for nutrients. However, people under continual stress are more likely to try to manage their problem with alcohol, sugar, nicotine or caffeine, substances that not only damage the cells and impede the brain's biochemistry but also affect its ability to successfully deal with stress itself, thereby creating a self-destructive pattern.

To maximise the well-being of your brain, it's worth following certain basic guidelines – not as a one-off, six-week diet, but as a lifestyle change, because what we are talking about here is giving yourself optimal brain function for the rest of your life. How badly you want it is up to you, but stay with it once you've started and you'll be amazed by the rapid improvement you experience.

The rules are simple. Blood doesn't circulate as freely when there is excess fat in it, so choose low-fat foods. Don't go on a starvation diet; just eat less and more often and stick to low-calorie foodstuffs, unless you can burn off the extra calories through exercise. The starvation diet is a dangerous option because it radically reduces blood-sugar levels – and the brain's only fuel is glucose. So when you starve the body, you seriously risk starving the brain, and in extreme cases this can cause permanent damage.

Finally, it's always worth remembering that the brain uses sugar and cannot store fat so, although you may sometimes be sorely tempted, it is technically incorrect to call someone a fathead.

Give yourself an upgrade

I am not an expert on brain function and I have never conducted scientific research. Nonetheless, I have seen at first hand many people radically improve their performances by changing the way they think about themselves, about their situation, and – critically – about their potential. For instance, often during my courses, people will tell me they are right-brain or left-brain thinkers. Now, if you study more detailed accounts of brain anatomy than this book offers, you will discover that there are indeed differences between some people's brains and others – differences that explain, for example, why women tend to be more intuitive and men more practical, differences which doubtless find their roots in genetic evolution. And, of course, I do believe that some people are *naturally* more musical, artistic or creative, than others. But just as importantly I believe that we all have the capacity to *develop* our musical, artistic and creative abilities. What stops us is believing we can't. But if you label yourself a logical left-brain or an emotional right-brain person you are restricting your ability to 'see' yourself as anything other than that.

To do any real justice to the physiological basis of this subject would involve my going into far more detail than would be appropriate here, but I hope that this chapter has given you some insight into why and how the brain functions as it does. I have added this chapter to give a sound scientific explanation as to why the seven principles are effective, but remember knowledge is not power, it is applied knowledge that is true power.

HAVING PROBLEMS?

If you're struggling to achieve your goals, here are some points that may help you out:

1 Examine if you are returning to old habits, thereby letting the old failure habit dominate your thinking.
2 Think positively. Overwhelm your nagging self doubt, with positive thoughts and language.
3 Remind yourself of the purpose that lies behind your goals.
4 Accept some days will be more challenging than others – don't beat yourself up over failures – learn from them and move on.
5 If you need to re-set the goal or plan – then do so, and put it into action now.
6 Do not shy away from problems – tackle them face on.
7 If you are having feelings of self pity or low self-esteem, take your focus away from negative feelings, and find opportunities to help others in some positive way, through practical help or an act of kindness. It will get you back on track.
8 Believe in yourself – that you can achieve anything you want to achieve. Repeat this belief every day.
9 Examine your attitudes – and make sure to choose the positive ones.
10 Keep learning every day something new that will help you succeed.
11 Laugh.

ROBIN SIEGER NEWSLETTER

The Robin Sieger newsletter takes a refreshing look at the universe of success and inspiration. Littered with innovative, informative and insightful thoughts and stories, the newsletter will help you to make sense out of it all and will inspire you to reach further and higher than ever before. More than 3,000 people worldwide already enjoy the benefits of this dose of good sense, good humour and good ideas, helping them to take positive control of their own lives.

To sign up for your FREE subscription please visit: www.siegerinternational.com and register online today.

KEYNOTES AND COURSES WITH ROBIN SIEGER

Robin Sieger is one of Europe's most in demand motivational speakers. A successful author and businessman, he is a gifted communicator, able to inform, inspire and entertain audiences worldwide. His talks motivate and push audience members to new levels of self-awareness and success.

Robin's company, Sieger International Ltd, aims to push the boundaries of organisational and personal performance levels. His mantra is 'Dream Big and Dare to Fail' and the training courses create change in beliefs, expectation, attitudes and results. Natural Born Winners is run as a two-day foundation course throughout the year for individuals, and corporate training courses focus on leadership, change and creating success cultures.

In addition, Robin runs an exclusive five-day executive retreat once a year, limited to seven attendees, and he also accepts individual clients for one-to-one coaching, limited to three per year worldwide.

Anyone attending one of Robin's keynote speeches will experience a range of emotions and will leave feeling moved, inspired and/or motivated, with the underlying message enabling them to built self-esteem and confidence, and to set more ambitious personal and professional goals.

To book Robin Sieger for your next conference, or to find out more about the training courses offered, please visit www.siegerinternational.com or contact:

Sieger International Ltd
T: +44 (0) 845 230 5400
F: +44 (0) 845 230 5401
E: bookings@siegerinternational.com

About Robin Sieger

Robin Sieger is one of Europe's leading authorities on success, motivation and peak performance, and a truly unique thinker whose ideas, initiatives and philosophy have guided people worldwide to make positive change and create personal success.

He is one of the foremost motivational speakers in the world, and was one of the first speakers in the UK to be awarded a Fellowship by his peers in recognition of his motivational and business speaking achievements. A gifted communicator, his humour, passion and compassion underpin the message behind his presentations, which are noted for their ability to simultaneously inspire, inform and motivate audiences to excel beyond their current performance limits, turning potential into profit.

Robin is Chairman of Sieger International Limited, a respected creator and provider of training and personal development initiatives, with offices in London (UK) and Charlotte (USA). Sieger's trademark programme – Natural Born Winners – enables personal and organisational transformation to begin, and inspire people to reach fullness of life. Clients range from start-up charities to Fortune 100 companies and programmes offered include culture and attitude change initiatives for major organisations, and life-skills training for schoolchildren.

It was following his experiences in overcoming cancer 20 years ago that Robin began to extensively research success, high achievement, and happiness. He believes in living life to the full, and sets himself a physical challenge every year to raise money for his charities. Robin's passion is for people, and enabling them to wake up to the world of opportunity, and much of his learning programmes centre on life mastery, self-leadership and making change happen at a personal level. He has dedicated his life to making a positive impact on the lives of others.

A TV series based on *Natural Born Winners* will broadcast in October 2004.

FOR FURTHER INFORMATION ON
ROBIN SIEGER AND SIEGER
INTERNATIONAL LTD'S SERVICES,
PLEASE CONTACT

Sieger International Ltd,
Molasses House,
Plantation Wharf,
London SW11 3TH

0845 2305400

www.siegerinternational.com

robin@siegerinternational.com